This book incorporates:

Everyday psychology for everyday people, living in an everyday world, doing everyday jobs!

It does not matter if you are rich or poor, you will still be living in the *everyday world* with *everyday people*.

Some books by Christine Thompson-Wells:

Selling Made Easy

Discover Your Selling Power

Making Cash Flow

39 Steps & 39 Days To Debt Recovery

Money Management For Students

How To Find Your Mind Of Gold

Adam's Mind – Eve's Psyche

The Psychology Of Money

And

Many 'How To' Children's Books

Christine only believes in writing books that have a purpose – her books are intended to assist people to become self-sustainable.

The purpose of her journey as a writer is to enrich the world of her readers.

ISBN : 978-0-9873523-0-9
Copyright © 2012 re-write 2017, 2020
including all illustrations belong to
Christine Thompson-Wells

Masterclips (1999) IMSI http://www.imsiuk.co.uk (UK)

All rights reserved.
Published by: Books For Reading On Line.Com Pty Ltd.,
Under license from MSI Ltd Australia
Company Registration No: 642923859, Australia

See our web site: www.booksforreadingonline.com

Or contact by email: sales@booksforreadingonline.com

BOOKS
FOR READING
ONLINE

Chapters   Pages

Do you have a *Passion* to learn, to grow and to be the person *You* are meant to be? If this is so, please keep reading.

Introduction
From The Author

We all need to develop self-sustainability. There are techniques to learn, know about or develop, in order, to live the life, you want to live, to release stress and to financially survive.

When your finances are intact, for the most part, your life stays within a manageable framework. However, when you are dependent on any other person or a financial income which is related to what you sell, and if you are not aware of the techniques you need to make those sales happen, you can very easily find yourself out of work, no income and with little prospects of finding work in a selling organisation.

Most businesses are about selling either directly to a customer or through agents. Business is about the exchange of something in return for cash, credit, or favours!

This book is about sharpening your mental skills which allows you to move and grow your 'mental zones' and to use techniques which put you in the winning seat. As you develop your skills, you will adapt, modify, and move forward, always knowing the next move to make; having this knowledge allows you to be constantly one or more steps ahead of your competition.

I'm a businesswoman, money psychologist, teacher, and writer. I have had my share of success, but I've also had to learn hard and devastating lessons to get me to this point in my life.

It is through my constant enquiry of how, does something work, or not work that allows me to put the words down on paper and produce the books I write. As a teacher, I cannot do anything – even go into business, unless I know there are benefits, not only for me and my family but for the whole community at large.

From owning successful businesses, a vocational school and spending many years at university, to developing new ideas in other peoples' businesses, I learn and grow and use this valuable information to pass on to my readers.

I've looked at other businesses and seen how, when a business is bought for a net $700,000 and over a three year period, can be developed to sell at a gross $3 million through using my own knowledge from my *'Centre of Intelligence'*.

I have given my ideas to people which have allowed this successful process to take place.

My ideas continually develop, this allows me to do the work I do; my purpose is to enrich people's lives both financially and in their wellbeing.

Wellbeing comes when you feel personal growth and the satisfaction of doing a good job. In any form of selling, you have the ability, to continually grow, create, and be rewarded for the effort you have put into the work you do.

My book *Discover Your Selling Power* allows you to take the position you are now experiencing; to work and develop your past experiences, combine the old and new experiences all of which add to your personal empowerment in selling and contributes to the growth of your *'Centre of Intelligence'*.

Christine Thompson-Wells

Chapter One

Discover Your Unique Selling Power

When you discover the Power of Selling it is a bit like turning on an electric light.

Like so many human behaviours, selling is complex and has many components.

I have identified at least *six components* when one person is selling to another, these being:

- The number of *things* being sold
- The possible *combinations* of things that can be sold
- The different *personalities* involved
- The *demands* made by the seller and the buyer
- The range of *principles* involved and
- The *purposes* of the buyer and the seller.

The things or components may work in many combinations and engage with many different personalities. The people involved will make different *demands,* will hold different *principles,* and have different *purposes* – all of this is the combination of one simple sale.

To become a successful seller, you need to constantly engage your brain and work with your mind. Selling is using psychology in the knowledge that 'if you don't understand human behaviour, you will not understand how to sell'.

It is about a person exchanging their money for things or services you have to offer.

Selling has *ten principles* as well as the six components every time a sale is made. During the sale process, you exchange information with your customer continuously.

Your body language and the words you speak are continuously monitored and the customer hears and takes notice of every small nuance. You try to give the customer an impression of:

- Honesty
- Relationship
- Trust and worthiness
- Genuineness
- Value in the goods or service you offer
- Warranty – it is going to work, so I won't lose out if it doesn't
- Purpose – I can see what it is for
- Benefits
- Outcome – I can envisage owning it, and
- Reciprocity

Your customer will quickly disappear if he/she feels any of the above is missing. It takes a long time to build the many impressions in just one single process so it is worth gaining more information in advance.

When you are building your repertoire of information, prior to selling, it's better to have a general background on peoples' habits, dislikes, likes and other general information.

Let us look at each of the principles separately.

Honesty

- Honesty is a basic human instinct and not all sellers are honest with their customer/s.

Case Study 1 – The Rip-Off Merchant

Background

For a number of years, Cheryl had worked hard, writing her books and was looking for a *road-to-market.*

The Study

Cheryl worked in nursing and wanted to start a new career. As a little respite from the work, she started to develop children's characters she later worked into books.

She gradually wrote a number, of children's books and wanted to start her own publishing company.

She found this difficult to accomplish as the publishing industry has its own approaches and there are people who know the 'ins and outs' and people who are trying to find out how to learn those 'ins and outs!' Cheryl was one of the second group. Despite constant attempts she found it almost impossible to establish her business.

Cheryl networked fervently, going to business breakfasts, lunches, and meetings whenever she could. At a business lunch in the heart of Surrey, England, she met an agent for, what appeared to be an international *Angel Investment Company* for people with feasible ideas. Cheryl became interested in what the agent had to tell her and went home and spoke to her husband about the chance meeting.

A few weeks went by and she thought some more about the agent; she made contact and the wheels started to turn. She firstly had to hand over £400 for a CD containing information about how the organisation worked: it said, 'the organisation had people in many walks of life, with wide and varied experiences in many areas of the business world from the financial sector, holiday homes, publishing, idea development, banking, science and technology and many other fields.'

After Cheryl and her husband had worked through the CD, they thought about the process.

The next phase of the development required them to send over a three-month period, three amounts of £4,000 (about A$30,000). They thought long and hard and eventually decided the fee sounded reasonable in exchange for support, guidance, contacts in the publishing world and investment to the value of £50,000, as the documentation promised.

After Cheryl sent the money as requested, she waited patiently for the next part of the process to happen and waited; the Angel Company was based in Australia.

In a phone call to them, she asked for the strategic plan and the contact names she had been promised. The Rip Off Merchant 'promised to send an email with this information'.

The email arrived a few days later, it contained nonsense on a couple of pages – the information was worthless and did nothing to advance her business.

Later, a contract arrived requesting her to assign to the Angel Company, the copyright in all her work, the titles of the books she had written and the titles of those she planned to write in the future!

Cheryl was a bit smatter than that; she didn't sign the document and on later investigation found that she was not the only victim in a string of fraud activities. The 'Rip

Off Merchant' and his company were under Federal investigation in Australia.

- Honesty is integral for you to become effective in selling.

Relationship

- Many professional salespeople, and marketers build good relationships long before they approach a customer or client about buying.

This relationship with the customer can be built through genuine care and consideration. If a person does not want to buy, do not push them to buy; build their relationship first. It is said, *'it takes at least three contacts with a prospective customer to build the relationship;'* it might take more!

If a person is undecided about buying, and they buy under pressure, research has shown there are always negative repercussions to the sale.

---

* Many Angel Investment Companies are set up to help and support other people with good ideas. They contribute in either: money, knowledge,e and contacts; most organisations want some form of security to support their investment. There is a cost for the service and legal documents are signed. Each person using such a company, needs to do it with legal advice.

> A good measure in any relationship building is to test yourself: at the end of the first interaction with the new customer, measure your success rate out of ten!
>
> 1 2 3 4 5 6 7 8 9 10

I am always impressed with the power of the human mind. Try this exercise, it works every time. Surprisingly, you will get an answer. You may not get it right away, but you will get one. Sometimes you get the answer you do not want but listen to what your mind is telling you.

When you want to sell goods or services, there is always a purpose attached to the relationship. It might be:

- To please another person
- To satisfy a need: to eat, to quench a thirst
- To fix a leaking tap
- To express emotional, feelings for another
- To satisfy a personal emotional state.

A woman having a facial as a treat is pleasing an emotional state: she wants to feel good and usually justifies her feelings by saying: 'I deserve it'. She probably does if she has completed a task or done something exceptionally good; or it might be just a treat. Whatever the reason, it is her emotional state which is the driving force. The same may be said of a man treating himself to an expensive pair of shoes – every sale made has an emotion driving it!

Each of these purposes listed above is motivated through a person's Emotional Intelligence - I will talk about this vast topic in Chapter Four.

Trustworthiness

It can sometimes feel difficult to trust people, especially if you have encountered a 'rip-off merchant' as in case study 1.

Trust has many elements attached to it; it includes:

- Faith in another person
- Belief in that person
- Confidence they will always do the right thing by you
- Conviction that you almost feel you would give your life for
- Reliance on the reliability in another person
- Being able to depend on another person
- Being able to count on him or her

Being able to confide in them and know what you say to them will never be spoken about to another person and being certain of that person.

Trust has your soul in the feelings you have about another person. Once it it established, trust goes so deeply into a person's psyche that it is almost unreachable. When trust is broken, it is almost irreparable.

When you are selling, building trust involves more than exchanging money for an item or items, it takes you and part of your soul to complete the transaction. Thus, to become a successful seller you will need to allow the buyer to build their trust in you; it's a big ask, but it must be done if you are to be successful.

Genuineness

Are you genuine about the product or service you are selling? Your genuineness will always show through if you really believe in your product or service. Being genuine means:

- The product or service is real and does what it says it will do
- It is authentic and not a copy of someone else's product
- What you say is true
- The product or service is the actual thing, or it is a mock-up of the real actual thing, if this is so, say so
- It is not adulterated in any way

- The product is legitimate and not like the above case study.

Value

The value relates to other things within a range. The perceived value may not be the actual value. The actual value is set when an item, or service is bought by another party, the seller and the buyer agree on the price, and that price is paid. Often land has a perceived value that is not the actual price that will be paid for it when a sale takes place.

Case Study 2 – An Opportunity – Taking advantages of a recession

Background

Buying and selling can be a difficult process when the item is large and there is emotional pressure to sell. The emotional pressure and love for other people can lead us to forego vast amounts of money, but we do this in order to meet the commitments we have – this was the situation facing a young couple who needed to sell their house on the outskirts of London, United Kingdom during the world recession that followed the 2008 banking crisis.

The Study

There are nearly always winners and losers in selling large items such as houses, motor vehicles, jewellery, pieces of art, businesses, and companies. When you are a loser in the deal, the item being sold is large and you stand to lose a large amount of money, it 'stings' and hurts your very being.

A young couple needed to move back to Canada in a hurry; the elderly parents of both were sick; but they needed to sell their London home. The opportunist, a man in his mid-40's, noticed the family home when it first appeared for sale in 2008. There was a bit of movement in the British economy in 2009 but not much and the housing market slipped downwards quickly. Most sensible people were prepared to 'sit tight' and see what the future would bring. In 2010, the market was still sluggish, and people were still reluctant to buy large items.

But as their parents' health deteriorated, the couple needed to sell their lovely home urgently.

The market slumped even further, and 'time was of the essence' to sell up and move overseas. The agent arranged a second viewing for the prospective buyer.

The price had dropped from £650,000 in 2008 and it was almost settled at £500,000 from the 'opportunist.'

However, he made a second offer of £475,000, which price was verbally agreed by the owners of the home. Then, yet another phone call from the house agent saw the price chopped again to £460,000. With the deterioration in their parents' health, they agreed to the price.

Quietly, the young couple confirmed to each other, that '...we will not go down one cent in price again and if we can find another way to keep the house we will do so'.

The residue left in their minds was of distaste and, seething anger and the feeling of having been 'done over' financially. With the house sold, the couple returned to Canada and in time to say their farewells to the remaining parent.

The opportunist needs to have, all his, or her ducks lined up and it is only by chance that he or she can make a killing.

Many investors work this way. A recession hurts many people. A recession is caused by a collective framework of thinking and greed. Although the actual assets are still in the community, their perceived value has become fantasy. Assets might become toxic – the gap between their perceived value and their actual value is too vast to bridge, as in the practices of Lehman Brothers, the world's fourth largest investment bank which filed for bankruptcy on 15th September 2008.

The destruction caused by a few greedy people looking for large financial gains is felt by the smaller businesses and individuals. There will always be opportunists to take advantage of all situations; you would need to settle with your conscience where you stand on this one.

Warranty

People always feel easier about spending money if they know there is a warranty supporting the sale. Your warranty is how you stand in their perception: 'if it fails, they have some form of comeback!' If you are selling something of worth for its true value, a warranty further endorses the item's price.

Offering a warranty is cost-effective. Research shows, that very few items are returned under a warranty or guarantee and, if they are, it is because the item has a genuine fault, or the complaint is genuine.

Purpose

If people can see a purpose for buying, your job is made easier. When a person is 'looking' they possibly intend to buy. The sale might not be made immediately but the possibility is there. For people to give you their valuable time to look at, listen to, feel or discuss what you are selling, there is always an ulterior motive behind the interest they are taking – they could end up being the best customer you have ever had. There are *five types of curiosity* which a person might display in giving you time:

- Simple curiosity
- Fascination of your product or service
- Intention to buy at a later-date
- Questioning – will your product or service satisfy their purpose, or
- They are just killing time - yours as well as their own.

Benefits

There is always a reason for somebody to buy a thing or a service. The reason is that 'somebody, somewhere needs or wants what you have to sell'. There is always a benefit (perceived or otherwise) attached to every sale you make; without a benefit being attached, the sale would not go through. Benefits are emotional, and feelings of satisfaction, and come in various forms:

- 'I feel good'.
- Allowing the person to express their emotional wishes or desires.
- Making life easier – buying a new kettle after using a saucepan to boil the water in the morning.
- Allowing somebody to take a mental holiday – buying a two-door sports car when they have a family of four and two dogs!

- Realising a dream – a cruise of a lifetime; these sales relate to high emotional drivers, feel good expectations and individual dreams.

A benefit perceived or otherwise, may only last a short time for the purchaser, but their choice to purchase your goods or service is a process of elimination for the buyer. A buyer will always have the question at the forefront of their mind: *'…..what benefit will I get if I buy this?'*

Outcome

There is sometimes a period, after the purchase, during which the customer is allowed, to change their mind or think twice about what they have spent their money on. This is a 'cooling-off period'. If a large purchase has been made such as a sports car, the buyer of the car might realise how totally inappropriate the purchase has been (to meet the family needs) but decides to keep it anyway!

Perhaps over the next five or so years, he/she will only take the occasional look at the gleaming sports car as it sits in the garage. Or, the purchase is a pair of Jimmy Choo shoes, which are worn once or twice; the owner can always say, 'I own a pair of Jimmy Choo shoes!'

This type of buying has pushed the button of a particular ego state within the purchaser and the seller has been fortunate enough to make the sale at the right time, with the right product; it could be a 'sale by chance' and does not necessarily show that the seller has perfected his or her art in selling!

However, it is not the 'one-off' sale that usually makes a successful seller wealthy; it is the repeat selling. As a seller, you want your customer to use, eat or wear what you are selling as quickly and as often as possible.

Consuming your goods or service ensures repeat sales.

Case Study 3 – Kellogg's Corn Flakes (Elliot, 1994)

In 1981, Kellogg's (in conjunction with its advertising agency, J. Walter Thompson) decided to place an advertisement on as many breakfast tables as possible by printing the advert on 1 million milk bottles. The milk bottles of Unigate Dairies had an average 'life' of 28 trips, so advertisers estimated advertisements would reach 3 million doorsteps, on average 9 times. (Cardwell, Flanagan 1999).

The study revealed that, new customers were not encouraged to go out and buy Corn Flakes. People who already ate Corn Flakes, however, made 17% more purchases of the product after seeing the advertising on the milk bottles.

Reciprocity

Robert Cialdini describes reciprocity as a fundamental law in human society. It is the feeling of obligation that binds societies and communities together. Reciprocity also allows the seller to sell.

Goods that satisfy basic human needs will sell throughout a recession. Such products are used in everyday living and some carry well-known brand names.

Such Items Are:

- Bread
- Milk
- Potatoes
- Meat
- Fish and foods such as cereals
- Flour and baking ingredients
- Condoms
- Sanitary wear
- Laundry detergents
- Bus fares and
- Petrol/diesel etc.

Reciprocity is not necessarily seen by the consumer when a country is in a recession. A case in point: when fruit and vegetables are sold above the accepted price and before the recession then the goods are sold at an exorbitant price.

When items rise above a certain price, say apricots at $9.00 (£4.50), most people would think twice about buying them, in or out of season!

Luxury items are not at the front of the mind when money is tight. Knowing how people think and behave will allow you to make sales under difficult conditions.

In Chapter One there are Six Components you need to consider when selling, try with recall, to list the six:

1. ....
2. ....
3. ....
4. ....
5. ....
6. ....

The next time you sell or buy something, take notice of your actions and words. Also take notice of the actions and words of the person you are buying from or selling to.

Your Notes

....
....
....

There are many cognitive elements working in your mind as you try to make a sale – it is understanding how your mind works within the knowledge you have that makes the difference. Selling is an exciting area of any business, but it is a science and can be measured.

Chapter Two

Your Mental Operational Mode

Many people tell me they are experts at selling when they apply for employment. However, many of these people do not know the first thing about selling.

As I have said, 'selling is a science'. Selling any item or service can be measured. The ways or techniques used to sell the item, or service can also be measured, as can sales of individual items, or individual services.

Predictions of selling items or services can also be made and those, too, can be measured. The Stock Market is no more and no less than the selling of commodities, goods, or services and both the predictions of the Stock Market and the sales made, are measured globally at a detailed level.

The Tax Office measures sales by businesses and individuals.

All numbers can be measured, and all measurements can be done using different approaches, different measuring tools and technology. Therefore, if you are selling, your performance can be measured and the measurements can be used as data, giving predictions and outcomes – selling is therefore a science.

Selling is a process of growth and elimination and therefore, if you are selling for a living, you, your company, and your competitors are measuring your performance – *this is why* – selling can be investigated.

To be successful in your career, you need to have a full knowledge of how the system/s work or do not work. You need to know how to make-adjustments and modify your behaviour, and approach to meet the demands you are presented with. Once you have the knowledge, you can take a realistic yet strategic approach to any situation. When you increase your negotiation power, you can itemise each scenario before a move is made or a question asked – that is pure mental empowerment.

There are many people in sales who don't know how to approach a customer or client, they are completely oblivious to the job they are employed to do and wonder why, after a very short time, they are again, 'looking for another job!'

If you are armed with information and you have developed your *'Mental Operational Mode'*, you can, not only get work, but achieve goals that are far beyond most people that don't have the skills and information you possess.

The fascination of developing skills that become 'life-skills' is that, once they are developed, they don't cost you anything to travel with, you don't need permission to use them and they belong to you.

'Life-Skills' give you added benefits all through your life; you can keep building your skills' and, in turn, a skill or skills can become unique to you. Not only can you build a better lifestyle for yourself, but the development of skills allows you to create financial opportunities that once were not available to you.

From a brain surgeon to a florist, from an accountant to a charity worker, we are all selling something in exchange for money.

Let me explain more: a brain surgeon is selling, to his patients his knowledge, expertise, time, and skills in operating on the brain. The patient, with the brain condition goes to the brain surgeon whom he or she hopes will cure the condition. The patient not only wants to be well but is also putting into his or her mind the outcome of the operation – becoming well again and living life to its full capacity.

However, held within this thinking is far more than just the outcome of the operation. The patient wants assurance of the best outcome possible; he or she also wants to feel in good hands and that the brain surgeon can do all he or she is claiming or known to do. Within this mental framework the patient would need to feel comfortable, emotionally secure with the brain surgeon and happy to go ahead with the operation.

The patient's emotions are driving them when they decide to go ahead with an operation – nothing more and nothing less.

The scenario of the brain surgeon is not unique. In every sale which is made daily, the world over, we have the 'brain surgeon scenario'.

Whether the sale is small – only a dollar, pound, or euro – or at a corporate level of multi-millions exchanging hands, through countries or continents, the 'brain surgeon scenario' is the background.

It doesn't matter whether it's a child buying an ice cream or a pensioner buying a grapefruit or potato at the supermarket, in the minds of the customer/s there is constantly a *'buy or not'* analysis taking place.

In any buying or selling situation there are individual 'mental frameworks' or *'mental operational modes'* exchanging information. The exchange of information and the minus or plus of the numbers in all currencies constantly takes place around the globe, in different market categories from banking, to the butcher or grocer, from the board room of Shell or HSBC, to the person on benefits – each and every individual's mind operates in a slightly different way. This is why, buying and selling can become confusing at times...

As discussed above, sellers are in every walk of life: even the ironing lady is selling her time to do somebody's ironing.

Sellers Include:

- Investors' in the rental market
- Investors' in stocks and bonds
- Bankers' – banks sell money or *'proposed'* money in transactions
- Car sales' people
- Local mobile hairdresser
- Supermarket owners or investors'
- Department store owners'
- Small shop owners'
- Gardeners
- Ironing men or women (you do other people's ironing for a living)
- Dentist and doctors
- You sell your time and skills to your employer – therefore, you are a seller as well as an employee. You become a 'buyer if you buy goods or services back from your employer.
- Property developers' and many more.

Any person who sells something is a seller. This looks easy to understand or is it?

The way the human mind works in buying and selling is a minefield. Whether buying in the corporate world or buying personally, lists of buying and selling can always be drawn up.

Listed below are just some of the factors involved when a human being is about to buy anything at all or spend money:

- Past experiences
- Current needs
- Current wants
- Money available
- Time constraints
- Emotional states including:

  -desire to please another person
  -personal feeling of pleasure at succeeding in doing this
  -feeling more secure when succeeding in doing
  -feeling good – 'this purchase will fix everything!'
  -the purchase will satisfy emotional needs but not all and
  -personal ego is boosted by the buying – this feeling may be short-lived.

For the seller similar factors are involved but driven by a different paradigm:

- Past experiences

- Current needs
- Current wants
- Price range (s) within which to sell or not sell
- Time constraints
- Emotional states including:

  -need to financially survive
  -need to match or surpass others
  -need to be a leader and not be left behind
  -need for recognition of success by one's peers
  -need to be secure and not feel threatened and
  -need to work within their own framework or *'Mental Operational Mode.'*

To achieve your own *'Mental Operational Mode'* of working will take considerable work on your part. It's not just the reading you need to do but the internal work on your own:

- Thinking
- Attitudes
- Perceptions
- Habits
- Lifestyle and
- Actions.

This all means you will change in some areas of your life.

Thinking

A thought can be the start of an idea. It takes many thoughts to formulate ideas. From ideas, concepts grow – a concept is a collection of ideas and this is the foundation of **NOW** and into the future.

Attitude

If a child develops a negative attitude at an early age, unless the child (or later the adult) changes that attitude, it can be with them for life.

A negative attitude can destroy personal growth when it interferes with your:

- Latent talent (the talent within every person that needs to be discovered – this sometimes takes personal work and dedication to discover)
- Self-esteem
- Life success
- Job or educational prospects
- Relationships
- Satisfaction with yourself
- Personal growth
- The ability to see an opportunity and
- The ability to *make an opportunity*

A negative attitude develops a *'Loser Mentality'* within the individual. At, the moment of birth, we are all born to be winners.

It is the development of every person's individual life environment from:

- Within the family home
- Personal experiences
- Personal outcomes associated with personal effort
- Mentally encoding information
- Personal perception and the
- Internalisation of information

The above develops either a negative or a positive attitude to life.

The one good thing about having or owning a negative attitude is, you can always change your way of thinking and behaving, (change your mind set or your *'Mental Operational Mode'*). That alone is a great asset for all human beings.

It can already be seen how many variables can exist in any, one, personal *'Mental Operational Mode'*. The art of selling is complex and is yet another area of investigation you need to understand if you are to be successful in your working life.

Achieving life success should not be seen as a pathway full of misery and hardship but as a pathway full of challenge, discovery and personal growth; this is the type of growth that will take you from mediocrity to wealth and personal satisfaction.

Perceptions

So many times, you hear a child say: *'...when I grow up, I'm going to be ....!'* How often does that child turn out to be you as an adult?

As children we all have perceptions but growing up and the experiences of adult life can sometimes leave us 'battle worn', exhausted and just wanting to sit and let the world go by. Sitting and letting the world go by will last for a short time but, sooner or later, you need to get off your butt, and be accountable to your life and the way you live.

If you have had some 'knock downs' in your life it may be because your perception, at the time, did not take-into-account your talent, skill, knowledge, attitude or experiences. Perception is a collection of intangible thoughts and need to be respected but not always acted upon. The wrong perception of yourself, your ability or your achievement can leave you 'high and dry' when you are selling for a living.

Habits

Habits like attitudes are thinking and actions in one way and only that way. Cleaning your teeth a particular way can be a habit; the way you wash the car or stack the dishwasher can be a habit; 'does it annoy you if anybody does it differently to you?' These are habits that do not always give you the best outcomes for your investment of time, effort, blood pressure or stress.

Developing habits in selling, such as ignoring a customer who is waiting to be served because you have a job to do, that you consider to be more important, is bad indeed.

How many times do I see people doing this in my own business – a great number? And yet it is as difficult to break another person of bad habits in my own business as it is within their own personality should they choose to make the changes.

It is only by, each, and every individual, taking ownership of their own positive development that changes happen for a better outcome. The first thing I do when I see a customer being ignored is: I develop an education program to meet the situation and face it head-on. If you know you have bad habits and they are holding you back, face them and put positive action into change for the better *'Discover Your Unique Selling Power.'*

Lifestyle

Your lifestyle is dictated by your income and wouldn't it be nice to be able to dictate your own income and then live the lifestyle you would like to?

By gaining knowledge and information you will put yourself in this winning position – you will be able to set your own terms of employment, life reference, the accomplishments you want to achieve and the challenges you want to face without fear and have the ability to live the way you want to live.

When people choose to 'lock their mind away' it's sad for these people, but it is their place and they have taken ownership of that place; it's not until they choose to change that they will be able to change! They have indeed, made a 'mental contract' to stay where they are. There is more about contracts in Chapter Four.

You may be selling loaves of bread at a supermarket today but, with a different attitude, way of thinking and working, you might be running your own business in six months' time.

With positive changes made:

- Your sales improve
- Your attitude takes on a new and positive dimension and you may be offered the first step up the corporate ladder.

If you own a business, you may take the business in a new and positive direction.

Positive changes happen in your life when you make positive changes in your mind.

Actions

Of course, the human mind is the driving force behind all human endeavours – even the shirt on your back was once just someone's thought many years ago, but the thought was adapted and the idea grew until it became part of the fashion of the 21st century. The chair you sit on took a similar route or gradual adaption to the current version you use today.

Endeavours include putting thoughts into ideas, ideas into action and action into creativity; developing all of this in applying materials to make the shirt or the chair you now own. Positive actions give positive outcomes.

Case Study 4 – The Dynamo

Background

Many people have great ideas; they can be dynamos in any business. On a daily-basis, ideas, work within the human mind, and yet many ideas are left to rot away. Staff who are ideas-based are worth their weight in gold.

The Study

A lady who works in one of our shops is an ideas woman. She sees what is happening in the shop, she listens to the customers and then she organises her thoughts into ideas, she considers her ideas, then speaks to other staff members and, usually, her ideas are adopted. Nearly, all of her original thoughts, go to ideas to successful outcomes in developing a new product, re-arranging systems to work better or re-organising work schedules.

She pulls many 'plusses out-of-the-bag' for the business – she is a very valued member of staff. She is a woman of positive action and it shows in her work and her relationship with the customers; she is always working within her *Mental Operational Mode.*

Your *Mental Operational Mode* is critical to the role you play in life. You can choose your Mental Operational Mode: it is the choice you make and the framework of reference you choose to work within. You might choose to keep your Mental Operational Mode in low gear and do little or nothing in your life, or notch up the gears and work to achieve the life you've dreamt of, to fulfil your dreams.

Managing the challenges is yet another learning experience and adds to your repertoire of skills and knowledge, - that challenge, in order for you to grow, is sometimes worth the pain and growth which it demands to reach your full potential.

✳✳✳✳✳

In the following chapters, I take you deeper into how your mind can become the best friend you have.

The human mind is a tool that is overlooked by almost all educational institutions – both public and private, within higher education and within many work environments.

If managers, employers, and educational authorities took a different approach to the human potential surrounding them, the country and the world would become a better place. Having said that, individual growth is the responsibility of the individual, that means you are responsible for you....!

Your Mental Operational Mode incorporates the performance you exhibit when selling.

Developing Life Skills is an important process in keeping your Mental Operational Mode in shape.

Note one Life Skill you have developed over the last six months – it may be:

- *Learning to drive*
- *How to make bread*
- *Understanding a complicated computer course which gives you work and other skills – skills which enable you to move up the corporate ladder or enable you to be more selective in the work you do.*
-

Your Notes:

....
....
....
....

Many people die without realising the power held within their own skull.

Your 'Mental Operational Mode' works with you 24/7 – it does not charge you for the service it offers and all that is needed is a little work from you.

If you want to go somewhere in life, achieve what you want, you will need to take the initiative and do your homework to reach your destination.

Chapter Three

Your Mental Operational Mode Is Connected To Your Mental Toolbox – Your Powerhouse –
Use It!

It continually astounds me how many people working in sales live a life of limitation, when all that is needed, to get more out of life, is to learn how to work with their brain and mind.

Working with your brain and then your mind does not cost any money, there is no money up front; this mental tool is constantly in your head 24/7 and has been since almost your conception.

People die and even in their final days do not realise that they could have gone from poor-to-rich in just one thought.

If you are selling for a living, all it takes is just one committed and positive thought to change your whole situation from negative to positive.

The human brain is a tool that is the receiver, processor, and transmitter of information. The brain is central to the human nervous and physical system; it is what makes you, You. Your brain, however, is not your mind!

Ten per-cent of the human brain is made up of neurons and the rest of blood vessels and glial cells (glia).

Glial, comes from the Greek word for glue and simply put, glia is the glue that helps to keep you thinking, asking questions, and seeking answers. The important role of these cells wasn't discovered until the 1960's (Koob, 2009). They work with neurons, and act as insulation for them – glia gives neurons room to move, and to remain healthy and functioning properly. Because you are selling, you are constantly interacting with other human beings, so if your glia is not working properly, nor will you be fully harnessing your selling power!

The food you eat can interfere with your glial cells, which means that your lifestyle can reduce your income. If you do not understand how your brain is working, it will be difficult to sell and reach your selling potential.

You Are A Seller - Your *Mental Powerhouse* is connected to the food you eat!

As a teacher, writer, lecturer and business owner, every day I see people who own brilliant minds and waste the very essence of their being through a lack of understanding of the *'powerhouse'* of the mind they are working with. This is one of the reasons I continue to hammer these words onto pieces of paper.

The human brain needs to be looked after. The most eminent scientists continue to research to help us understand how to work with the brains we own. These few words are just that, a few words, but they are a starting point for your continuing research into how your brain works.

If you do not eat the right food, you cannot expect your brain to work well. If people realised that what they ate can affect their selling power, they would think twice before letting some food pass their lips. At this point one has to ask: 'why is some food called food when it clearly does not feed us properly?'

Some over-processed foods are in fact poisonous to the human body and brain, so they are not food. Food is meant to be a nourishing substance eaten, drunk, taken into the body to sustain life, provide energy and promote growth. However, some processed food has been shown to do otherwise.

Normal fatty acids have a natural curve to their molecular shape. These molecules can fit together in vast numbers with enough space remaining so the structure functions at its best. However, if these same fatty molecules are changed by manufactured processes, or are heated for long periods (as in deep frying) in fats or oils that have been modified they alter into a form rarely found in natural foods or in nature.

The molecules are different, they are straighter and narrower, and no longer have their original curved shape.

These distorted and altered fats will pack more tightly together within the cell membrane, making it more saturated and rigid – less flexible and less able to function properly. These altered fats are called 'trans-fatty acids.' The damage to the processed food we eat is impacting on the human brain structure like no other since the evolution of the human species. (cited Franklin Institute, http://www.fi.edu/learn/brain/fats.html)

Because we are the instruments of now, future children may be the ones that suffer the effects of these products.

For the sake of our children and our own personal futures, we need to become aware of the food we eat. We also need to take stock of 'Now'. If you miss a sale or were 'slow off the mark,' you need to ask the question: 'Did I miss out because of the food I've eaten?'

How it works

From the above you are aware of the processes that changes the shape of the molecules of the natural fats in the food to 'trans-fats'. To operate successfully, your body and brain need whole food, that is minimally processed, non-fatty, and definitely not, *over-sugared, over-salted or deeply fried.*

When a brain is starved of food that contains the vitamins, minerals, and nutritional value it needs, you feel:

- Under-the weather
- Exhausted
- Unable to concentrate
- Lethargic
- Sluggish
- Indolent
- Mentally heavy
- Lazy
- Drained
- Lacking in inspiration
- Unwilling to think about how you feel.

In such a condition, new ideas are difficult to come up with, and putting your thoughts down on paper is too hard. You are in what psychologists' call 'avoidance' – you avoid the inevitable and resist the challenge of something new.

Lateral thinking is beyond you and negative feelings and lack of positive action start to crowd into your life.

These are just some of the effects of a starving brain that will affect the power of your mind, your *'mental powerhouse'*, your 'selling power' and, invariably, your income.

When the brain, glial cells and neuron connections are working they send electronic messages to other parts of your body: 'move your limbs' or 'turn your head.' Messages can become confused, so you make a wrong move. The wrong move might result in an accident or saying the wrong thing at the wrong time just as you are about to 'seal a deal' in a sale. If you can remember this happening, think back to the food you had eaten over the 48 hours before and take note of foods which might not have helped your brain and its functioning.

From our physical evolution (possibly 2.4 million years ago) to the 20th century, there was little deliberate input of preservatives, colourings and other additives to our foods and drinks. Nothing in our past-history can be compared with the contamination of food over the last 40 to 50 or so years.

The fast-food industry and the major food corporations have modified and developed various foods until much of the original substance of the food no longer exists.

The modification of some foods and drink is not good for the operation of the human brain and contributes to some of the mind's messages becoming mixed, tangled, or confusing for the owner to understand.

People experiencing such a reaction, cannot understand simple tasks or instructions given to them because of what they have eaten or have previously swallowed.

The intake of added preservatives and the combinations of different processing methods and food additives interferes with your brain's activity and limits or completely restricts your understanding of simple instruction. In the workplace this has been a factor in some industrial accidents, absenteeism, performance, and failure to accomplish sales.

Many people become the victim of the food they eat, as the teenager in the next story demonstrates. Becoming aware of this and asking, 'is this food good for my brain and the operation of my mind?' is a good starting-place if you want to improve your selling performance.

Case Study 5 – Your mental energy starts with the food you eat!

Background

Eating the wrong food or swallowing the wrong drink will give negative outcomes in the actions you do and the words you speak. The combination of wrong food and drink can and does cause a disturbance in your thinking and can later hinder your future.

The Study

Early one morning I did some emergency cover for a teacher at a school in the United Kingdom. It was a large class of about 28 pupils. We were only just starting the lesson when, I realised I had on extremely disruptive student in the class.

The student was male, aged about 14. Being early in the week, the students were trying to settle and get into their schoolwork. The disruptive student was at the back of the room. He tried to settle, but when settled, would instantly become disruptive again. He would jump up from his chair and start making loud comments, blame other people for what he was doing and so on. His comments and actions were out of keeping with the classroom environment which, overall, was relatively quiet once the students were working.

I went to his seat, spoke to him quietly and tried to reason with him and settle him down. Almost instantly, as soon as my back was turned, as I went back to write information on the white board; he would start again. By this time, the other students were becoming annoyed, even angry at the disruptions he was causing in the room. I too was angry and now said, 'your disruptions are unacceptable, please leave the room.' As I finished speaking, the student threw a large bottle of drink across the room, narrowly missing my head in its flight. With the noise, both the Assistant Head and the Head Teacher arrived to see what was going on!

The student was ordered to leave the room and go to the Head's Office. I filed a 'bad behaviour' report, describing the incident. I also recorded the name of the beverage the student had obviously been drinking. After some hours, he resumed classes, only for a second more sever incident to happen with another teacher – the student was later expelled from the school.

When treated properly and with respect, the human brain then the mind has a large capacity for learning and achievement. The individual mental capacity of people, I believe, is immeasurable.

However, the brain is a muscle that works with and for the human mind. Like all muscles, the brain needs good, whole, natural food, and to be exercised on-a-daily basis.

Exercising the brain comes through learning new information, building new skills and working to stretch the brain daily, not weekly, monthly or in one-off exercises! The brain needs regular workouts, it needs stretching and pulling until it cannot do any more for the time being. It is only when your brain is taking in new information or you are learning how to build new skills that your mind starts to work hard and for you.

When you have worked hard with your brain, you feel tired, and need to take breaks to replenish the energy levels that allow you to continue operating.

If people only realised that every mouthful of food they ate was vitally important to their *'Mental Operational Mode'* and that lack of the right food and lack of exercise were indeed interfering with their income, they would think twice about their current position in life and where they could end up in the future.

It is not just the incorrect food you eat which interferes with your thinking and mental capacity; also:

- Stress
- Lack of rest
- Tiredness (short-term)
- Fatigue (long-term)
- Alcohol
- Smoking and
- Drugs

We are all different and different foods, drinks and habits work on your mental states in different ways, this is discussed in Case Study 5.

I don't know if the fizzy drink was the cause of the problem or whether the student was taking other 'mind-altering' substances, but the outcome for the people observing such behaviour was unsettling and extremely disruptive to any work that needs to be completed.

The person, who is experiencing the turmoil, might not have any idea what the fizzy drink or other substances can do and are doing inside their heads. Not only does the mind-altering substance affect the brain (and the mind) but it travels through the entire bodily system, possibly doing other damage to organs and cells.

Your Powerhouse

The foetus of every living, healthy person starts the same. The brain stem develops around three weeks after fertilisation. From an early stage, the brain starts recording information. This recording of information allows the baby to put down some small memory blocks or banks.

From that age, you have been learning, recalling, and adding to your world of information. You collect the information by moment, record it, discard some but keep what you consider interesting in your 'memory banks'. Importantly, recall is essential in most employment roles' and, is definitely so, in selling!

A memory bank is the storage place for your collected information and can become your 'powerhouse' as you recall your customers' needs, wants and desires. The more you recall about your clients or customers, the more successful you will become. Customers are always impressed at the information you retain in your mind when you are relating to them.

The brain has three defined and distinct parts: the upper outer layers of the left and right hemispheres (also known as the cerebral cortex) and a part known as the cerebellum or the reptilian brain (MacLean 1973, 1982)

It is vital to your career that you understand how your brain is the *'centre of your intelligence'* and how its processing controls your central nervous system.

The brain is a large, complex organ in which pathways or neurons, (briefly spoken of earlier,) transport information from one region to another – to keep it simple: it is your internal road network.

When you interfere with your brain through the food, drugs, or drink you take in, this adds to the stress your brain and body experience, and once your brain is under stress you find it harder to think logically or relate clearly to the tasks you are doing or attempting to do – including selling.

Diagram 1

When question marks fill your mind and you are having problems understanding incoming information, always

go back to your food and drink intake over the last forty-eight hours.

As I have mentioned, your brain consists of three vital parts. These parts work together forming one brain. However, each of the vital parts (also known as separate brains) has unique and crucial work to do for you; they work on some separate areas but also in harmony with each other.

If any part of your brain does not work, this is shown in the actions you take, through movement, voice, or your understanding of a situation. Without becoming too medical, we need to focus on the person who wants to work in sales and to get the best from their input and performance output.

Some people in the medical profession have understood how food works in the human system for a number of years, but the information isn't known to the general public nor is there an understanding of the vital role food plays in education and within schools or colleges.

Knowing about your basic food intake is vital to your well-being and your success in any career.

The body and brain like a combination of foods to work with. By eating complex carbohydrates, you can increase your mental capacity and work over longer periods of time without feeling fatigued, tired, or irritable.

The magic held within these foods is their ability to give your blood the amount of glucose that allows you to sustain energy and have the vitality your body needs.

How It Works

Complex carbohydrates are foods that are eaten as whole foods without being broken down or over-cooked; uncooked fresh fruit is one complex carbohydrate. When eaten, your body works to break down its fibre and extracts its nutrition.

Once the food passes from your mouth and into the stomach and gut, your body does the work.

The complex carbohydrate in fruit contains fructose and valuable vitamins and minerals. The islets of Langerhans' within the pancreas control the amount of sugar going into your blood. Once processed, the natural fructose becomes your blood glucose, which is vital to maintain energy. Your body works for you and will only allow the right amount of glucose into your blood. This amount of glucose is governed by your body and your energy levels.

Because your body works hard to breakdown complex carbohydrate, little residue is left to make you fat.

Processed foods contain excess sugars and fats that are stored as fat on your body. This is where complex carbohydrate wins out over both processed food and straight carbohydrate which includes over-sugared food.

With trans-fats (fats that have been broken down and their molecules altered from curved to straight), your body doesn't have to work hard to gain the unwanted weight, which sits on your hips, stomach, thighs, legs and arms with its residue of cholesterol being stored in your veins and arteries, waiting to give you a heart attack at the time you least expect it.

Heavily processed foods just breakdown to leave quantities of toxic deposits such as fats and sugars in your body, shaping the way you look, feel, think, work, and react.

If you perform badly in sales, you may need to look at the food you eat.

The sales world is extremely competitive and there is always somebody waiting in the wings to pick up your valued customers – they are there watching and waiting; they are the 'predators' and cannot be blamed if you are not in peak condition! It takes one wrong move to lose a sale.

Case Study 6 – The lost sale

Background

Joe had worked with a computer company as their sales director for many years and knew a range of people in the field. He had also worked extremely hard to try and secure a large, multi-million-dollar order that was being put out for tender and would come up shortly. Joe would present his company's profile, brief, costs, and completion dates.

The Study

It was the night before the presentation to the corporation and Joe thought he was ready. He and a colleague went out for dinner; they had a meal and a few beers – harmless you might think?

With a combination of exotic foods, a light sprinkling of monosodium glutamate (E621) sprinkled on the food by the chef to enhance the flavours, and the extra beer, Joe was up through the night with a bilious attack. The next morning, he had a bit of a hang-over! Needless to say: Joe's performance in the presentation had a lack-lustre' quality!

The minute he started to present Joe knew he was behind the 'eight-ball'. He seemed to go from bad to worse and slowly he saw his efforts drift away into the ethers.

Joe's competitors won the contract and Joe returned home feeling angry with himself and his performance, not to mention the bonus he missed out on.

Joe's bodily reaction to the night before is fairly, typical of the human system coming under attack. Feeling sick, was Joe's body trying to repair itself. The bilious attack was the attempt by his body to cleanse his systems of the toxins he had eaten and drunk.

In the above case study, I have only mentioned the body; the human brain also suffers when the body is under attack. Joe possibly had a headache and other physical side effects (such as feeling sluggish and being unable to think clearly). He might have found it difficult to show the cutting edge of his work and other benefits his company could offer to the project.

All the work done by Joe and the team in preparation for the seminar was wasted because of the interference, the tangled and mixed messages his brain and mind were trying to work with.

All of this could have been avoided by a little work on Joe's part and by Joe staying in control of his situation.

The performance in your sales career is always a reflection of your inner health and well-being.

It is true that, some people can sustain a high energy output even when eating rubbish, but sooner or later there will be a negative consequence.

Proteins and your performance

Proteins are as important as complex carbohydrates for your body's good functioning but again, the protein you eat needs to be understood.

Main proteins come in the form of meat, eggs, some grains, and fish. Fish is by far the best brain food around and is high in Omega-3 fatty acids. Had Joe eaten a light meal the night before his presentation – for example, steamed fish, some lightly cooked potatoes and green vegetables – his performance would have been a lot sharper and he might possibly have achieved his desired outcome.

The way your protein food is prepared and cooked can interfere with your performance level. Protein breaks down in cooking, so a well-done steak will contain little goodness. Accompanying it with deep-fried vegetables may do more harm than good to your performance.

Alcohol has no protein: it is pure, adulterated carbohydrate containing large quantities of sugars, some preservatives, and other modifiers, each of which interferes with your brain and mind, thus, possibly hindering your performance at a vital time.

If you are to give a presentation (as in Joe's case), avoid anything that will hamper your performance, hinder your thinking, or restrict you in any way. Joe's performance would have been sharper had he taken more notice of the messages his body had sent him over the years.

Your mind and body constantly send you signals about what is agreeable and acceptable and what is not. Your measuring gauge is the way you feel after you have eaten or had something to drink – it either agrees or disagrees with you.

When something you have eaten has made you sick, simply left you feeling sick and from that moment you cannot face eating or drinking the thing again, you have developed an 'aversion' to that drink or food.
'Aversion' is a natural reaction by your body; your body is working with a signal sent from your brain through your 'messaging service' which is actioned through your nervous system.

A previous experience, that you recall sends the message through your feelings and you remember the feeling of the sickness experience at that time.

'Aversion' messages are powerful and should be listened to.

Over the years I've studied students in high school, tertiary education, young offenders' in correctional centres, employees, managers and owners in business. There is a definite connection or correlation between the food they eat and the performance levels they achieve.

From the above, there is also the combination of habits the person creates and the boundaries they lock their mental capacity into.

More about your brain and exercise

Your brain is a marvellous tool that costs you nothing and gives you everything, and yet, most people don't acknowledge their brain, their mind or indeed, that, they have these components working for them at *no extra cost*.

Your brain is your servant and is waiting to serve you. From the sales executive to the three-year old who is going to kindergarten for the first time, the brain is waiting patiently and for every command.

Whether you are in sales or in any other profession, your brain needs exercise and so does your body. Athletes know and understand that, through exercise, they perform better. The same is for salespeople, teachers, the clergy, butcher, baker, and the candle-stick maker; the Pope and the Queen need to exercise to keep their brains at peak performance.

To clinch a sales-deal you need to keep your mental metal sharp! You need to understand that, without bodily exercise, your brain is only working at a fraction of its strength or capacity.

You now understand the importance of the make-up of your brain: how complex carbohydrates work and, the role that protein plays. To bring it all together you need to understand that your brain also needs good doses of oxygen.

When you are working hard, working to tight timelines, even with the right food intake, you can still fall short when giving a multi-million-dollar sales presentation. You will use up large quantities of energy and oxygen when the pressure is on.

Pressure builds up carbon dioxide in the human body and, though you want to go faster, work harder and do more, the build-up of carbon dioxide will slow you down. The human body needs to do regular, physical exercise for all the components to come together: giving a presentation that allows you to win the deal.

The components are: understanding the way your brain and mind work together, that the food you eat, the drink you drink also have an impact on the way your brain and mind work; the exercise you do affects the levels of carbon dioxide and oxygen you have in your blood.

Joe had fallen short of his target, not because he had not previously worked hard, but because he did not have a complete understanding of how his body would react to the different way he had treated it.

Had Joe eaten a good, whole balanced meal the night before the presentation, gone for a walk after the meal instead of drinking alcohol or even done some light exercises, he might have been light years ahead of his competition.

Oxygen is taken in through the breath you inhale. When you are under stress, you will breathe lightly and not expand your lungs as far as you need to or take in the quantities of air your body requires. When you are under pressure, you do not exhale properly and so you slowly build up the carbon dioxide levels in your blood.

Gradually, this build-up of carbon dioxide interferes with your brain and thinking capacity. Your thoughts and your 'messaging service' may become tangled and you might not give clear responses to the questions you are asked, the words you speak or the actions you take might be the wrong ones.

Oxygen is needed to keep your blood clean and flowing. With this clean and flowing action, your brain works to its maximum, supporting your mind giving you sharpness and coherence in your responses to questions and situations.

Exercising is a positive way to keep your oxygen levels balanced and at the right level, and helps you to digest your food, which in turn supports your brain and allows your mind to work. Exercising allows you to easily learn new skills which add to your *Mental Toolbox*. It keeps your *Mental Operational Mode* in good working order and your *Mental Powerhouse* working constantly with you, thus, moving you forward with every thought you have and action you take.

Your Mental Operational Mode is connected to your Mental Toolbox, which is your Powerhouse – Use It!

Over the next week, take note of the food you eat and while eating it, ask: 'is this food good for my brain, mind and will my body get any benefit from it?

The Food You Are Eating!

Day One..

Day Two..

Day Three..

Day Four...

Day Five..

Day Six...

Day Seven..

Your Notes:

....

....

....

Eating the right food, understanding the ingredients of what you drink and gaining insight to how these react on your brain and mind will help you to understand your performance level.

Plus, taking time out to recognise the effects on your selling performance will allow you to gain a winning edge in the work or selling you do.

Chapter Four

Connecting Your Emotional Intelligence To Your Mental Operational Mode, Your Messaging Service And Discovering Positive Magnitude

Emotional Intelligence is more widely understood now than at any other time in human history. As a school subject, 'Emotional Intelligence' within the discipline of psychology is widely accepted in the United Kingdom but sadly Australia is lagging-behind!

Children and adults constantly use their 'Emotional Intelligence.' Like all human behaviour, it is inherent and in each of us, and develops as we grow and mature.

What is Emotional Intelligence?

Charles Darwin identified the importance for survival of emotional expression (Emotional Intelligence) and the ability to adapt to the environment. Originally, Emotional Intelligence, was linked to cognitive characteristics of the human mind, such as in memory and problem solving. Moving rapidly through its history, this concept has also become the work of many influential researchers.

Thorndike (1920) used the term, 'social intelligence' to describe human behaviours in managing and working with other people. David Wechsler (1940) described 'the influence of non-intellective factors on intelligent behaviour'.

Howard Gardner's work went further in his book: *'Frames of Mind'* (1983), he introduced the idea of Multiple Intelligences. Further, he explored, the *'intrapersonal'* (the ability to understand other people) and the *'interpersonal'* (the ability to understand oneself).

Wayne Payne's thesis: 'A Study of Emotion – Developing Emotional Intelligence' (1985) enhances the theory and these concepts. A later book by Daniel Goleman (2000) added to the theory 'by exploring, traits and ability (trait being a characteristic, inherited or otherwise, of the person).

Salovey and Mayer (1990) describe Emotional Intelligence as 'the ability to perceive emotion, integrate emotion to facilitate and understand emotions and to regulate emotions to promote personal growth'.

The idea of Salovey and Mayer let us go even deeper into the subject allowing people in every-day life to understand why we do the things we do and say the things we say as a seller.

Emotional Intelligence will allow you to:

- *Perceive emotions:* understand body language including facial expressions, hand gestures, mannerisms, actions, and verbal cues in the customer.

- *Use emotions:* rapidly think things through, (using your cognitive ability), adapt and modify your reaction to every different selling situation.

- *Understand emotions:* use your knowledge to feel the emotion you are experiencing, work with its complications, understand that emotions are constantly changing in both you and your customers and that every situation arouses a new set of emotions.

- *Manage emotions:* rapidly examine negative and positive situations both within yourself and others, modify the situation, regulate it and bring about a 'Win-Win' outcome.

Emotional Intelligence is as old as human evolution. It arose when humans realised they could think things through and that: *'....if I do this, the outcome will be that, while if I do that, the outcome will be this!'* This was when the connection was made between thinking, emotions and the action or in-action that took place as a result.

Had this realisation not occurred, we might still be living in trees or caves. The human being has developed the power to reason and identify problems and find solutions. It was the merging of human thought and behaviour (actions and reaction, stimulus and response, cause, and effect) that made human beings different from other species. This, too, was the beginning of human psychology. Becoming aware of how you work with your Emotional Intelligence, you go through many choices.

Whenever, you are confronted with 'choice', you start to put down 'mental markers'. You are reasoning, you are measuring and processing information. Buying and selling includes the stages of:

- Choice
- Option
- Selection or preference
- Range and lastly
- Decision

As a seller you are steering your customer through the above *markers* while they analyse:

- You
- Your product
- Your manner, style and approach (these vary slightly with each person and the rapport you develop)

- Your appearance
- Your genuineness, honesty, and truthfulness (each of these points will measure differently with different people)
- Your attitude
- Your knowledge
- Your presentation of your product and use of the venue
- Your capacity to meet their needs and wants and lastly
- Your pricing and pricing structure.

Notice pricing is the last point the customer looks at or indeed considers when they are genuinely buying. They are not necessarily interested in price if you are satisfactory in all the other criteria. If you do not meet all of them, they may lose interest before you even get to the price.

The above information is going through the customer's mind while they are speaking with you.

Within three seconds they have made up their mind; they are comparing you with other people, other products and the current goods or services within that marketplace.

The window of opportunity is small, just three seconds or shorter, so you need to be well prepared in advance for the opportunities that come your way in that short time.

Your customer(s), future client/s are working with their Emotional Intelligence, within their Mental Operational Mode and with their mental tools; they add the information you have given them to their 'Mental Toolbox' or collection.

This information leads to the choice the customer eventually makes. When action is taken there is always an outcome, they buy or do not buy. The customer also has the alternative of going to spend their money somewhere else!

So, by accumulating the knowledge of how your mind works in selling you learn that:

➢ You and your customer have thoughts this leads to an idea – a single idea can lead to many ideas
➢ The ideas may join up and build to create a picture
➢ You put action into the idea and the actions become part of the picture, which in turn prompts
➢ Outcomes which might be changing the way you think about selling your product, taking a different approach to the way you present your product, even altering the way you present yourself.

Ask yourself:

- Are you prepared to think about making changes in your life?
- Are you prepared to read more?
- Are you prepared to change your way of thinking?
- Are you prepared to take on new ideas and give them a go?
- Are you prepared to make changes in the way you look and present yourself to the world?
- Are you prepared to do the extra work such as going to college or taking on self-improvement programs?

Of course, there are many ways to make changes; just 'yes' to one or two of the above would indicate you are looking to make a positive difference in your life.

The world of selling is all about impression and the above list is just that; it's a list that asks: 'are you prepared to change the impression you give?

It is the impression of your goods or service that you leave with the customer that is going to make you either successful or unsuccessful.

Each person's individual impression of you is different; you may please one person but thoroughly infuriate another – this may go back to each person's (the customer or client's) individual perception and life experiences which include background.

In order to be a winning seller you will need to become ultra-sensitive to the people around you and especially the people you are selling to – when you are in-tune with and sensitive to the people and the environment you are working among, you are working with your:

- Emotional Intelligence, using your Mental Operational Mode and you too are collecting tools for your own Mental Toolbox.

Regardless of age, from a child buying its first ice cream, to a mature executive making a million or multi-million, dollar purchase, they are looking for the next clue or piece of information that will enforce their buying choice. The executive may think: 'will this choice make a positive difference to me and will it make a positive difference to the people in the company, and ultimately, will this increase my income and wellbeing?'

From child to adult

A child is looking to satisfy a 'need' or a 'want' they have identified. The child's experience is shaping his or her mind for future growth in buying and selling.

Children need to identify 'needs' and 'wants' from an early age. They also need to have an understanding of how their mind works and how to respect their brain and the way they use their mind when information is put before them - a child buying an ice cream has identified a *pleasurable want.*

The company executive is working from the remnants of information he/she has collected from childhood. The remnants have been continually modified, adjusted, re-shaped and added to.

You can see here, that if a child is given the wrong information at an early age, their 'Messaging Service' may become tangled and they will not be equipped to take the necessary action to manage or cope later in life.

Your Messaging Service

I have briefly spoken about the three inter-working parts of your brain: the left and right hemispheres of the cerebral cortex and the cerebellum. From about three to nine weeks after your conception, your brain has been collecting information for you. This information slowly forms the 'Messaging Service' that interacts with your feelings – your 'Emotional Intelligence'.

The Left and Right Hemispheres and the Cerebellum
The right and left hemispheres sit under your skull; the cerebellum, (hind brain or reptilian brain) sits at the back of your head under your skull.

At birth, your brain is fully equipped with almost all the neurons it needs to allow it to work. A neuron is a nerve cell that is the basic building block of your nervous system. Neurons work differently to other cells; they are the 'Messaging Service' that operates throughout your body and brain.

The neurons in the brain continue to grow after birth. Rather than, the numbers added, the neurons grow in thickness and complexity.

At six months of age, the development of the synaptic connections between neurons takes place. During this period there is a growth of glial cells (previously mentioned) and the myelin sheath is added to the outer sides of the cells, giving protection to the cell: much like putting your hand into a glove during the cold weather!

These highly developed nerve cells operate through and with both chemical and electrical information. There are two types of neuron: sensory cells and motor cells.

Sensory cells carry information to your brain – this is the information you receive from your senses:

- Seeing – through your eyes
- Taste – through your palate
- Touch – through your skin
- Hearing – through your ears and
- Smell – through your nose.

Motor neuron cells carry information from your brain to your muscles, which work with your limbs making your body move: sit down, stand up, drive the car, empty the rubbish and more.

Motor neuron cells carry information to your face which allows you to smile, lick your lips, scratch your ear, make a face, or poke out your tongue!

The action of motor neurons allows you to make the contact with your customer; sign the contract, hand over the keys to a newly bought home, face a court hearing and more. Motor neurons help with the answers you give by operating your tongue and other muscles to make sounds.

The muscles in your body only move because your motor neurons have transferred an order: 'move!'

When you do not give out the message you want to give out, you get the wrong outcome or reaction. Almost every action you take, or word you speak is transferred to another person; they become the receiver of your information and you are the transmitter; the same process of interaction between you and the customer happens continually, but of course, in two directions, when you give and receive information.

Within selling, the above processes happen time and time again.

Every word spoken, each action taken, relate to you and your customer and you are constantly using the power within your Emotional Intelligence to interact and communicate the message or information about the product, goods or service you are selling.

From an early age, you have learnt to put a value on the information you receive from other people (these are the people transmitting around you). Based on the value of this information, you either accept or reject it.

Some people have received more than their fair share of negative information and have found barriers in many aspects of their lives. Some people are incapable of selling because they give out mixed messages to customers and the customer ends up frustrated, unhappy, and walking away without buying.

Many sales are lost because either the seller or the customer cannot connect with the other person's 'Messaging Service' and this invariably results in mixed messages being given and received.

The value of your messaging service in sales

Sales

Keeping your Messaging Service clear and accurate is critical to your success.

If you are selling for a living and have problems in communicating and as a result, your sales are not happening or are slumping – you might have picked up mixed messages from an early age and you may find it difficult to relay clear information to your prospective customers.

If this is part of your personality, perceived negative information can become like a 'concrete block' within your thought processes. The 'block' may hinder or hamper all the positive avenues you are trying to take.

The 'block' can be moved, kicked out of your thinking, but this may take some work; however, it can be done.

Remember, the 'block' the thoughts and actions are working within your 'Messaging Service' and are triggered by your Emotional Intelligence and your Mental Operational Mode.

Case Study 7 – The wrong messages

Background

If a person gives out the wrong messages in the work place all manner of mistakes are made.

Natalie had invested little to nothing in her future and was looking for work; at another person's suggestion, she found some work. Then what happened?

The Study

When employed, before her children were born, Natalie had worked as a waitress or in other areas of the hospitality industry.

As the children grew older, she thought she would look around for some work. Like some women in their late 40s, Natalie had kept herself busy with her family and shown little interest in anything else apart from going out to play bingo, poker, and other 'fill-in' pass-times.

Her marriage had broken down several years earlier, but she was now living happily with her new partner of about six years.

With Natalie's background, she had little to offer employers. Times were tough, the 2008 recession was felt hard in Australia and her partner suddenly found he was out of work with few prospects of work coming his way.

Neither Natalie nor her partner had invested in their skill base; they had done little to make things happen or to advance themselves.

Natalie, did, however, manage to find some work in a small café and the owner decided to see how she went with a trial. 'All seems to be working OK, not great,' he thought at first.

Later, the same day, the owner tried to speak to Natalie about something, but she kept interrupting with suggestion on another topic. Then, later she forgot an order! The customer waited patiently for about half an hour and then approached the counter asking for his food.

Later that night, the owner thought about what had happened and was not happy. He had given Natalie a chance to gain work,'... her mind was obviously set on something else other than her job, and her communication wasn't good'– thought the owner.

Natalie clearly had a tangled and mixed Messaging Service in her mind that would send the wrong signals to her speech, making no sense to her work environment. As a result, she gave out mixed message and was not concentrating on the work she was being paid to do.

Now, the employer was faced with a situation he needed to do something about.

An employer wants investment to be made in personal development by an employee. An employer looks for:

- Friendly disposition
- Experience
- Background
- Willingness to take direction
- Education

- Courses completed and

The employer asks:

- What will they contribute to the business or organisation?
- What added benefit to the business or organisation comes from employing this person?
- How does this person work with other people?
- How good is his or her reputation?
- Will they work with the already established group? And
- Can they sell?

In case study 7, Natalie will possibly be looking for another job shortly. However, the employer has given her an opportunity and she can build on that experience.

Natalie has responsibilities to herself and her future is her responsibility. She needs to invest in her future and have something to offer any future employers. Natalie had little education but was still working with her Mental Operational Mode, and her Emotional Intelligence, although her skill base was limited.

Natalie's *Messaging Service* is rusty, but she can do something about it with some mind work, hard work and concentration.

Ninety per-cent of Natalie's job was to sell – forgetting a customer's order identified her lack of concentration on the job.

The power of Emotional Intelligence

Like the study of psychology, Emotional Intelligence has been grossly under-rated. It is an essential player in the world of selling, commerce, trading, banking, education, healthcare, within state and federal governments and all areas of human interaction.

Emotional Intelligence takes a role in every aspect of your life. From waking in the morning and looking out of the window to see a cloudy, rainy day to talking and being with your wife or partner and to doing your job of work.

Emotional Intelligence lets you know when you walk into a shop or office and pick up bad or negative vibes from the business. Emotional Intelligence guides you when you feel things are wrong or that you are struggling to find answers when none are forthcoming.

Emotional Intelligence is the measure that keeps you safe and the hidden voice you sometimes hear inside your head and wonder: 'where did that come from?' No, you are not going mad, when you hear the answer to a question, or you are given an idea that turns out to be a solution to your problem. You are indeed, at that moment, in touch with your Emotional Intelligence.

In selling, Emotional Intelligence is paramount if you are to be successful. Getting to know your Emotional Intelligence means working with your inner Messaging Service; this Messaging Service is much like a road network. The network has high streets and country lanes all attached to it. Every road has a connection point to another road or route, allowing its users to easily get to different destinations throughout the area.

The human brain is similar but of course not the same as a road network. If you can imagine the time before the road network, all that joined up human settlements were tracks, fields, and countryside.
Before the road network existed, there was a thought, a thought turned to an idea at different times in different countries. Actions were put into the ideas and road network systems were built.

There is a vast amount of research being undertaken with a view to collecting information about how the brain works. It is interesting to note here, that though the electrical pulses that relate information from one part of the brain to another part can be seen and recorded through 'computerised axial tomography' (CAT) scans, the human mind , as a working component, cannot be photographed or recorded. We will return to this in Chapter Eight.

After you were born and developed into a child and then an adult, you became increasingly aware of what another human being was thinking through the actions they took or the words they spoke.

Instruments have been developed that can delve into the brain and stimulate happy or sad areas of the brain, but again, we cannot photograph the thoughts and memories that make the person happy or sad. And yet again, we have hit on the area of Emotional Intelligence.

Emotional Intelligence is the key to understanding how you will react in different situations of your selling career, so let us now go a little deeper.

John Watson

In 1920

John Watson, a research psychologist was unable to gain a research post at any university in the USA because of the unethical approach used and the negative outcomes of his experiment known as 'Little Albert'.

At the start of the experiment, Little Albert was not afraid of white rats. Then, he was exposed to the loud noise of a steel pipe being banged close to his ear every time a white rat was shown to him.

Little Albert developed a morbid fear of the rat; he associated the white rat with the noise of the steel pipe being banged. The boy's parents complained about the experiment and withdrew him from the research before Watson had time to correct Little Albert's phobia.

The methodology used in this experiment forced Watson into the world of marketing with J. Walter Thompson. Watson rose from selling coffee to become the Vice President of the company (see Cohen, 1979). Watson applied rigorous academic research techniques to marketing and adopted the same approach to the corporate world as he had in the academic world, and the techniques worked.

It's from Watson's time that psychology has become increasingly involved in marketing, advertising and selling, so much so, that without some knowledge of psychology in the sales world, a person can be left almost unemployable in those fields.

There are four main areas that need to be understood to gain even the smallest understanding of how you use your mind when you want to sell something or make a living form selling or buying. These are:

1. Developing a need in the customer
2. Getting the product noticed
3. Getting the product purchased and
4. Behaviour after the purchase.

Developing a need in the customer

There is a lot said about 'needs' these days. When a need is identified by the customer, they are in 'buying mode'. A need can be measured by many different tools of perception.

You might perceive the need to:

- Look beautiful
- Satisfy the ego
- Dine out at a five-star restaurant
- Lose weight to look like the latest pop star
- Impress the neighbours
- Be the best dressed in the office
- Stand out in the crowd
- Drive a flash car
- Buy the latest fashion, or
- Send the children to the most expensive private school

If you can identify with some of the above, you will be aware these 'needs' set other people's' opinions and values as the first priority in your mind – they are not a need, they are a want.

Marketing techniques can cause a 'want' to be re-identified as a 'need' by the customer. It is the perception and impression, left in the mind of the customer that is going to determine whether selling techniques successfully capitalise on this or not.

Developing the 'need' is to give the customer a motivational message without their knowing it or becoming aware that there is a 'buy' message.

To bring this point home, in the 1920s the Joint Coffee Trade Publicity Committee developed a campaign that created *work breaks*. These breaks are now recognised in the 21st century as *official breaks;* they originally started out as a marketing ploy to sell more coffee.

Work breaks are now considered to be needed to maintain health, assist with better workflow, and allow employees to play and thus enjoy their work more, adding to higher production or output.

In another case study the manufacturers of popcorn tried to establish a 'need' for an occasional treat in the form of popcorn and Coca Cola.

Flash subliminal messaging was used in trials during a film at cinemas in the United States showing the words *'EAT POPCORN and DRINK COCA COLA'* (Brean, 1958).

Flash half-second messages were given to the audience during a film and the sales of popcorn and Coca Cola were measured; the study identified no conclusive evidence of the effect of these, as the film showed several shots of people eating and drinking during its showing.

This type of subliminal messaging is now banned in the United States and the United Kingdom.

However, psychologists have discovered that people can respond to messages without realising they are responding – this is a mild form of subliminal messaging. Subliminal messaging is still used in many forms and in lighter approaches.

Subliminal messaging can be seen in products aiding weight loss: pictures of people who have gained weight are compared with the now lighter image and '...it's all possible if you buy this product! is the impression given by the advert.

Though this type of advertising does not have written flash words, the incoming information is transmitted to the receiver in a similar way to flash words – both leave an impression!

Getting the product noticed

Getting the product noticed is branding the product. A brand is a unique symbol that becomes identified with the product on sale. The brand image (such as McDonald's Golden Arches) is easy to identify. This type of branding breeds a following of people who identify as part of a group, and the group nearly always stays together because the following has become a habit and habits are difficult to break.

Developing the habit

Having an identified symbol allows a business to grow through association alone. How do you, your company or organisation start to develop such an association? The association is a habit and once a habit is established it is difficult to change people from it – a habit is ownership of something, or in some instances: nothing.

It is said 'that it takes six weeks to form or develop a habit'. That is debatable but we do know from marketing research, that it is the continuous, adopted, buying habits of your customers' that makes you or your organisation rich.

If, for instance, you have a habit of shopping at Coles Supermarket, and, one day, you decide to shop at Woolworths, you may feel lost, uneasy, or uncomfortable. This feeling might arise because you have shopped at Coles supermarket for a long time. It may also be because you feel you are being disloyal to Coles when shopping at another supermarket. Another way that the habit of being loyal to Coles might manifest itself is through Coles selling its own brands, which installs 'value for money' concept within the mind of the buyer.

A customer who feels uncomfortable shopping at another different outlet has in fact developed a habit and personal contract to shop at a particular store.

An adopted habit of buying from you or your organisation will add to your brand power and create more market opportunities for you or your company.

When an advert is played constantly enough, it would be expected that the repetition alone would build a brand and brand power; but this is not so.

Building a brand needs mental processing by the customer of value and benefits to them. Repetition alone, will not build a brand or the brand power associated with the brand and its products. This mental processing is the analysis of:

- *'What's in it for me?'*
- *'How do I or my family benefit from it?'*
- *'If I invest time and money, will I see a change in my life?'*
- *'It makes me feel better when I buy from them because I know them' and*
- *The customer or client has taken on ownership of the emotional attachment they have developed.*

These are buying analyses that require the customer to be committed, to own the feelings they have when they buy.

Large department stores operate through this ownership factor. People like to shop at David Jones in Australia, John Lewis and Marks & Spencer in the United Kingdom, Bloomingdales in the United States, because they feel they are getting something better, value for money and they like the image of the store. The process of branding always needs to include the 'Me' factor and the *loyalty factor.*

All branding needs to stimulate the Emotional Intelligence within the customers' minds and the feelings associated with the product or service.

The 'aaaah' Factor

Walt Disney knew how to push emotional buttons with his drawings and in developing his animations. Disney developed Bambi, a loveable young fawn. The fawn had the '**aaaah**' factor, which allowed people to own a little bit of Bambi through their emotional attachment to the character, even though Bambi is just and will always be a drawing, or many drawings put together to form the animation. Disney, a genius of the early 20th century, has contributed to the technology used in films and electronic games manufactured and sold in the 21 century – because his ideas were and remain brilliant.

As an adult reading this, you may recall the motion pictures, the colouring-in books, and the associated Bambi merchandise. If this is so, test yourself (1 = weak):

How strong is your emotional attachment to Bambi?

1 2 3 4 5 6 7 8 9 10

The animation brings the character to life and the life of the character is taken as a token of love by the audience – the 'aaaah' factor is established and the market place can develop an insatiable appetite for buying a product when it has this element attached to it.

The 'aaaah' factor takes people to another place in their mind. It allows them to feel soft and loving and want more of the good feeling. The 'aaaah' factor is a mental stimulation package and makes people feel good about the world they live in and about life at that very moment – it can and does have a short lifespan.

Further research has been carried out by Stayman & Batra (1991), in which two groups of people were shown two different advertisements for the same product. One was just written information about the product and the second included cuddly, emotion-provoking pictures relating to the product. The second group showed an emotional response that aroused a 'feel good' feeling. This reaction aided recollection of the product and the individual members of the group took personal ownership of the product – a habit developed with individual members of the group that could assure long-term association with the advertisement and an increased demand for the product.

Purchasing the product

New products are typically difficult to launch into the marketplace. Not all new products can arouse the *'aaaah'* factor in the customer.

The customer needs to have or be able to develop a *mental hook* which connects to their 'Emotional Intelligence and the association of the product or service.

When car manufacturers launch a new model at a car show, young, shapely, scantily clad women in bikinis catch the attending males' eyes which are supposed to draw the attention to the car.

The car does draw the attending male attention, but the female models may contribute the *'aaaah'* factor and to the mental transaction which takes place. With recall, however, this may lead to a later sale – even in many years' time because the *'aaaah'* factor has provided the 'hook' within the mind of that customer. If this is so, the marketing and branding have done their job.

A number of new products can become successful when a product becomes fashionable or has a novel approach to it, it can be seen as having good market potential. Conversely, many good products die a quick death if the marketing of the product is not done properly in the first instance.

However, the 'imitation effect' is well known in marketing. Thompson (1984) identified 'Post-it notes' as having this effect. The new sticky note was first put out through traditional or conventional routes, such as supply stores; this was not successful. In Denver and Tulsa (USA), the dealers ran promotions giving away the little 'Post-it note; this became highly successful and the little sticky note is now used almost everywhere from schools to government departments, private homes and more.

Behaviour of the customer after the purchase

To survive, as a seller, you need to have repeatable customer demand. If you are selling, you need to create a constant demand for your products or services. Follow-up contact with customers is vital to a business and its financial survival.

Building loyalty with the customers is the first step in positive communication when a purchase has been made. Loyalty is a form of contract and can become a powerful tool when used with integrity.

Follow-Up, Loyalty – The car industry

Ehrlich et al., (1957) surveyed 125 men to find out more about men who bought new cars. The survey concluded that '...new car owners tended to read advertisements about the make of car they had recently bought more often than they read adverts for other types of car', (Cardwell Flanagan, Meldrum, 1996) For as long as he owned the car, the new car owner had indeed, formed a mental contract with the branding and manufacturers of the vehicle.

In the food business, McDonald's, KFC and other international fast-food outlets build loyalty by offering a continuously changing 'taste the difference' fascination in their products. They also, from time-to-time, offer 'give away' children's merchandise in the form of small characters, some related to the latest children's film. By these marketing approaches, they too, are trying to trigger the *'aaaah'* factor and 'imitation effect' within their branding, thus, creating repeatable and ongoing selling.

The Mental Contract

For successful transaction to be long-term, a contract (mental or written) needs to be adopted by both the customer and the seller.

Mental contracts are developed within the customer's mind-set when a business or organisation gives:

- Loyalty cards – (a bit old fashioned now)

- Follow-up invitations: book launches, after-five wine and cheese, free coffee for the day, free tickets to a popular sports match and more
- Good service and/or
- Perceived value for money.

Value for money is perceived when customers buy a cup of coffee: they pay more per cup because one seller is *perceived* to be the 'in-place' to drink coffee.

Value for money may be perceived in fashion branding, cosmetics, perfumery, and shoes in the sale of most luxury items such as women's bags, and shoes, or fashionable brands of men's clothing, toiletries, shoes, and cars.

Loyalty is built up through your customers' or clients' feeling comfortable at your place of business – you or your staff are not intimidating, are pleasant and helpful, the venue is clean and well managed and there is a completeness about the whole environment – *'it's a nice experience for your customers or clients'.*

The above are all forms of contracts which any business can develop.

Many contracts are formed daily on a daily basis and yet little do we realise that at the time of buying a coffee or saying, 'I'll ring your later!' a contract has been adopted and a response is awaited by another person. The person is possibly your customer, client, or future client.

When you agree to buy something, you enter into an unwritten contract; contracts in any form are binding either through your code of ethics, your Mental Operational Mode, which relates to your mental state and ownership, or through it being written down in a legal document.

When a customer breaks a mental contract, it can be totally destructive to the person wanting to make or advance their sales careers.

If you look at the contract between the customer and Natalie, the contract was sealed when the customer ordered his food; he then patiently waited for his food to be taken to him at his table. Having to ask for his food about thirty minutes later, though, he seemed happy enough at the time it would have left a residue within his mind and the question in the café owner's mind: 'Will he come back?'

Natalie was possibly ignoring the rational part of her Emotional Intelligence – 'you need this job!' She did not stay in charge of her thinking – her thoughts were going in other directions. Her Mental Operational Mode should have been set to 'work' - she did not exhibit this.

When you understand how your Emotional Intelligence is connected to your Mental Operational Mode, that mode works with Contracts you make daily (written or otherwise), and you develop your knowledge, you increase your Selling Power. We can all gain by using the skills and knowledge we have. We can also add to what we have by working with 'Positive Magnitude.'

Positive Magnitude

Positive Magnitude is the mental awareness of building on the good knowledge you have and making a conscious effort to add one good learning outcome to your knowledge base each day.

There are 365 days in the year, multiply that by the next ten years and you will have learnt a lot and gained great volumes in your knowledge.

With each new learning you do, you relate it to your selling career, your home, personal or family life, your future career or in building your skills and skill base.

When you develop your Positive Magnitude you become empowered, you not only learn one new thing each day but the learning you are doing gains in exponential personal growth.

Natalie was possibly ignoring the rational part of her Emotional Intelligence – 'you need this job!'

She was not aware of how Positive Magnitude could take place within her personal growth.

If she had been concentrating on the work she was meant to be doing, she would be-in-charge of her thinking, and the customer would have received his order on time.

When you understand how your Emotional Intelligence is connected to your Mental Operational Mode, and how your Mental Operational Mode works with the Contracts you daily make (written or otherwise), and you develop your knowledge, you increase your 'Selling Power.'

Through using Positive Magnitude, this enforces you and you become empowered which in turn increases your ownership of your Emotional Intelligence and the life you live.

Working with your Emotional Intelligence in Selling will allow you to achieve more when selling.

Now ask yourself:

1. *Are you prepared to make changes in your life?*
    [Y] [N]
2. *Are you prepared to read more?*   [Y] [N]
3. *Are you prepared to change your way of thinking?*
    [Y] [N]
4. *Are you prepared to take on new ideas and give them a go?*   [Y] [N]
5. *Are you prepared to make changes in the way you look and present to the world*   [Y] [N]
6. *Are you prepared to do extra work such as going to college or take on self-improvement programs?*
    [Y] [N]
7. *Are you prepared to dress sharper to look the part?*
    [Y] [N]
8. *Are you prepared to change and to mentally move forward?*   [Y] [N]

Your Notes:

....

....

....

We have discussed in this chapter your Emotional Intelligence, Mental Operational Mode, Your Internal Messaging Service and the discovery of your Positive Magnitude.

In the following week, test and measure the following:

Note a time and place when you realised you were working with your Emotional Intelligence and monitor the differences you experienced.

....

....

Note and pay attention to your Mental Operational Mode – what did you experience?

....

....

How did your Internal Messaging Service work with you and what was your response to what you learnt?

....

....

By applying Positive Magnitude to your work daily, you can increase your knowledge exponentially, are you doing this?

....

....

Please keep a record of your progress.

....

....

Chapter Five

Selling Is More Than Just The Exchange Of Money For Goods Or Services

When you sell any product or service for a living, all aspects of your personality are used to make the sale happen. You draw on the framework you construct out of your:

- Uniqueness
- Expertise
- Knowledge
- Personality
- Appearance
- Attitude
- Disposition
- Charisma
- Appeal
- Intelligence and
- Approach

Uniqueness

Your uniqueness is a marketing tool that is constantly available to you. Singers like Mariah Carey, Beyoncé and others are known, not just for their voice but for their uniqueness. Each, and every person is unique, and we all have the responsibility to find this, sometimes hidden, part of our personality.

Expertise

Expert knowledge is essential to make a sale – you must know your product before you can sell it. If you lack information read up, ask questions, research, and equip yourself with useful information; it is essential if you are to be employable: you need to be an expert in the field!

Knowledge

In order, to do your job, it is your responsibility to know what you need to do the job! Why should an employer offer you a job if you have little or nothing to contribute? If this applies to you, why should you be employed?

From the chief executive to the person packing bread on shelves; in selling any product, a person needs to know what they are talking about. A person, packing bread on shelves would need to know the types of bread on sale, most of their ingredients, their shelf and eating life, the weight of each loaf or bun and any other, extra benefits it offers the customer.

An executive needs inside information about the product or service the company is offering, what and where the competition has an edge or superior product or service, and what can be done to make the product he/she is selling gain 'selling power?'

Executives need to develop their own 'marketing strengths' and to discover other external knowledge that supports their product. Even historical background is of importance – knowing how something has evolved, developed, or been manufactured are all assets in selling.

Personality

Many people in sales lack personality; they give little out in terms of warmness and friendliness; their whole demeanour is frosty – Salespeople need to be:

- Friendly
- Caring
- Happy
- Concerned
- Able to look customers or clients in the eye
- Have the ability, to isolate their personal life to and not take their personal life into the workplace
- Able to manage and work with all types of customers and different situations, and
- Respectful of both customers and of work colleagues.

Appearance

It is said, that *'the first impression is a lasting impression'* and this could not be truer than in selling. Customers or clients will be deterred from giving you their business if they perceive any of the following about you:

- Dirty
- Untidy
- Dishevelled
- In-appropriate in dress or décor of the business
- Scruffy
- Appears too old to do the job or out-of-date. With care, personal appearance can be made to look up-to-date and sharp
- Tired, hung over or
- Slovenly.

You, your business, and your organisation need to appear:

- Bright
- New
- Refreshing
- Friendly and warm
- Organised
- Co-ordinated
- Professional
- Contagious – 'their success will rub off on me'
- Infectious – the message of your business carries far and wide like the Virgin group of company messages do.
- Enthusiastic, and
- Colourful – colour is often underestimated when applied to the science of selling.

Many studies have looked at colour more from the artistic point of view than from the practical question of how colour can trigger sales in the marketplace.

The colours yellow and red are believed to signal that something is cheap – being opposing colours on the colour spectrum they make people look and take notice, so they have some virtue for the salesperson.

Blues and greens are cool and receding colours. This may make it difficult to sell products, for example, if these colours are too dark and heavy (dark-blue, dark-green), or used inappropriately in the packaging, and especially if they do not represent colours associated with or emotionally connect to the product!

Emotional connections are made to a product through what it is believed to represent. Most colours in the spectrum have an emotional attachment tied to them. This attachment is culturally rooted within the communities in which you grow up. Some colours are appropriate to communicate a particular message in one culture but may be totally inappropriate in another culture.

Red and pink can be used to represent love – red is worn by the bride in Indian and some Asian wedding ceremonies. Black has traditionally been associated with funerals in Western culture, it may also be associated with fashion.

The funeral directors, White Ladies in Queensland, Australia, conduct funerals by women wearing white outfits and white Stetson sun hats. After the funeral, each mourner is given a white flower to place on the coffin or throw into the grave. The White Lady concept is soft and pure in its approach which is a sad event for relatives and loved ones.

Apricots, shell pinks, turquoise and other mixed colours appear to be good selling colours. The fashion industry and paint manufacturers are always good indicators of the latest colour trends, so follow these if you find colour difficult for you to work with.

Attitude

The attitude of the CEO, manager, directors, owner, operators or employees of any business in the private or government sectors shows through to customers or clients – any false impressions that are given out are picked up by the customers through their Messaging Service and noted by their Emotional Intelligence.

The customer or client is continually reading sales people through the actions they take, the mannerisms they use, the facial expressions they wear, their appearance, the words they speak and the knowledge they have of the products they are selling.

Attitude and its connecting culture runs through every business and a negative attitude in one person can poison the business, from government departments to hospitals, and care homes, to schools, from garages to the local fast-food outlet and others – a positive attitude is paramount in selling through to developing and maintaining a positive business image.

Disposition

The disposition of people is often overlooked in interviews *for job positions. In you have a 'rotten disposition' it will* eventually be identified – get rid of it as soon as possible.

A bad or negative disposition shows in your nature:

- Character
- Temperament
- Temper and
- Outlook

A negative disposition gives you nothing back and will only take from you and leave you feeling depressed:

- You could lose your job or position.
- It can and does destroy relationships, and at the least,
- It leaves you feeling lost and lonely.

- You can be left in the cold when an opportunity appears.
- People will avoid you.

Your negative disposition shows through in your body language:

- Your head will often be slumped forward
- The way you walk changes – you do not have any *vim* in your step and
- Your face looks older and more drawn – age moves in and youth moves out!

Enough said – change for the sake of your health, wellbeing, and your financial future.

Charisma

Some people are born with charisma, some people develop a charisma as they grow and mature, but some people do not gain the skills to attract other people to them.

If you think you need to test your charisma level, do the eleven-question exercise below and examine your score. If you score between 6 and 10 on each of the first ten questions, this shows you feel positive about what you are selling; the higher the score, the more charisma you exude. This positive feeling will enhance your charisma and your own self-esteem.

If your answer to these questions is 1 – 5 this would show in your selling power: you will find it difficult to enhance your approach and your lack of charisma would be observed by your customer/s through their Emotional Intelligence and their Messaging Service.

You need to think about question eleven and work with some positive 'stress-free' time.

In answering the questions – 1 would be a strong 'No' and 10 would be a strong 'Yes'

1)   When you are speaking to people about your product or service, do you feel you have their attention?

1 2 3 4 5 6 7 8 9 10

2)   Do you find it difficult to speak to other people about the goods or service you are selling?

1 2 3 4 5 6 7 8 9 10

3)   Do you fully believe that the goods or service you are selling are value for money?

1 2 3 4 5 6 7 8 9 10

4) Do you think your personality helps you when you are selling?

1 2 3 4 5 6 7 8 9 10

5) Do the goods or service you are selling appeal to you and would you buy it (them)?

1 2 3 4 5 6 7 8 9 10

6) Do you feel you could sell your product or service to most people who showed an interest?

1 2 3 4 5 6 7 8 9 10

7) If you were having difficulty in selling your product or service, would you adopt another technique or approach?

1 2 3 4 5 6 7 8 9 10

8) When you have a new product to promote, do you take the initiative to research and find out more about the product or service?

1 2 3 4 5 6 7 8 9 10

9) Do you have to wait to be asked about the product or service you sell, or are you so enthusiastic about it you want to tell everybody anyway?

1 2 3 4 5 6 7 8 9 10

10) If you are out with your friends or family, do you find you speak about your work in selling or does work stay at work and home at home?

1 2 3 4 5 6 7 8 9 10

11) Please note, this final question is about you. Are you able to keep your work at work?

1 2 3 4 5 6 7 8 9 10

There are no right or wrong answers to any of the above. There may, however, be areas you will need to modify now they have come to your attention in particular with question eleven, a score of 6 and above means you give yourself 'time out', which is a good thing. A score of 5 and below would mean you are working too many hours in your head, so you need to take a break.

Appeal

All saleable items need 'Appeal.' From buying an island in the Pacific, a jet ski, a holiday, a fur hat, or a dozen eggs; each, and every item needs to have appeal. Appeal might reflect branding and is detected by every person's Emotional Intelligence and internal Messaging Service.

Appeal will:

- Attract
- Gain interest

- Fascinate
- Tempt people to buy

Appeal will please people's senses:

- To touch or stroke.
- To smell
- To taste
- To listen to
- To see and
- Have charm

It may be cute and cuddly!

When an item is appealing it is alluring and people are *fascinated* when something is appealing...

Intelligence

It takes intelligence to be a seller or buyer of goods and services – selling is a science. From selling banking to selling antiques, from selling fashion to selling a loaf of bread, all products are bought and sold because somebody – somewhere, has identified a need to buy or sell the item.

Buying and selling is not just about the exchange of money for goods or services, it's about meeting a person's, family, organisation's or group's wishes: to have something he, she, they, or it needs; or the desire to gain something more than what he, she, it or they currently have or own.

The intelligence driving the desire is generated through a 'gap' or 'hole' they have identified through either a single thought or many thoughts coming together. These have created the next step in the customer's mind and the desire to move forward and consider buying the thing they have thought about.

Simply put, if you are homeless and hungry, the next thought is to get something to eat and then look for shelter.

If you are running a business and are running low on the soft drink range you carry, you need to buy more soft drinks to fill the fridges and meet the demands of your customers.

The iron ore companies of Australia need to keep selling iron ore to China so its production can continue to maintain its highest performance.

If China's demand for the ore slows, so does its willingness to buy more ore and then the mining industry cannot justify keeping up production: jobs are lost, and people are unemployed. The loss of production trickles into the Australian economy and community, share prices slump, Australia's economy starts to lag, and the growth of the country and its mining companies slow down. World consumer demand keeps China in production – if world demand slows so will Australia's growth start to *slump.*

It takes intelligence to look for other markets and to put in strategies that allow for 'slump' in the marketplace. It takes intelligence to find another way of using iron ore and its by-products.

It also takes intelligence to know that there are 'saturation points' within any market and products can become superseded, outgrown, seen to perform worse than comparable products available elsewhere.

Watching the market and understanding the processes of human thinking will allow all sellers to become more astute and informed about market trends, human *wants, needs* and *demands.*

Approach

The first impression a buyer forms of you as the seller and the goods you sell (as previously mentioned) takes about three seconds. The buyer instantly looks, forms a global view and, from that one view, will decide to move forward and speak with you or move on to another seller.

Within those three seconds, the buyer's approach will also take- into-account:

- ✓ The first visual impact
- ✓ The instant messages sent through the five senses of the buyer:

1. **What they see** – the colour and presentation
2. **What they smell** – what they might taste (which might reflect what they smell)
3. **What they hear**, and
4. **What they feel** on their skin through touch
5. **The appearance**: is it clean, well presented and colour-co-ordinated or is it messy, grubby, untidy with little appeal other than needing a good clean and straightening up?

The approach to anything being sold is paramount in making the sale happen: wrong approach – no sale!

- Brochures need to be bright and glossy
- Written information needs to stand out and give a clean and uncomplicated message – straight to the point.
- Short sentence construction conveying one single thought – this brings even a complex message home
- Clean, clear outlines need to be used in both graphics and print
- Leaving 'white space' on any visual information can pay dividends

- Customers love a story and it's paramount for the story to leave them with the '**aaaah**' attachment – think hard until you find one
- The customer needs mental attachments and connections to positive information in the form of pictures, graphics, and written content.

The three-second impression also include, all of the above, but also the seller's:

- Body language: is it positive or negative?
- Manner: is it pleasing or upsetting?
- Knowledge: does he or she know about the product they are selling and what they are talking about?
- Warmth: is the seller approachable enough to allow the buyer to feel comfortable with them?
- As a seller, you need to establish whether the buyer wants to buy the product or service you are selling or just 'looking' and becoming familiar with your message?'

Framework

You need to work with and within a framework when you are selling. Staying with the topic involves knowing:

- More than you need to know about your products or services
- Their (it's) history?
- Their (it's) future?

- How to use (it) them?
- The material used to develop or make (it) them?
- Their impact on the environment – are there any environmental issues with (it) them? and
- The benefits to the seller, to the buyer, to his or her family, to the environment, to the community, to the country and to the world.
- Their depth: what is so different about your product that will make your customer want to buy it?

Can you quickly answer the above? If you cannot, I would suggest you do some homework.

If you are selling for a living, selling is fun and exciting when you sell to the buyer what satisfies their 'needs' or 'wants'.

Selling is exciting when you understand the complicated processes which take place during every transaction. Selling is exciting when you can *seal the deal* and know you have met the requirements of your customer which in turn, usually relates to repeat sales and can increase your own income.

Selling is more than just the exchange of money for goods or services.

To be able to sell, you need to be aware of:
1. *Your uniqueness*
2. *Your expertise*
3. *Your knowledge*
4. *Your personality and its effects on other people*
5. *Your appearance*
6. *Your attitude*
7. *Your disposition*
8. *Your charisma*
9. *Your appeal*
10. *Your intelligence and*
11. *Your approach*

Your Notes – what can you do immediately to improve your selling skills? Now write them down.

Your Notes

....

....

....

This chapter has spoken of a number of issues which affect sales and selling. We have discussed:

Uniqueness – how to use this?

Expertise – think of the difference!

Knowledge – what do you know?

Personality- how can you use it?

Appearance – you can make the changes

Attitude – you can modify your attitude

Disposition – you can move from a negative disposition to a positive with one thought

Charisma – you may need to work on your charisma!

Appeal – how can you add appeal to your selling power?

Intelligence – you can gain knowledge by reading more and

Approach – think a friendly thought and you will become friendly

As you work through this information you may want to add what works for you, what you have discovered, and the differences made.

Chapter Six

Your Mindset And Your Ten Mental Nuggets Of Gold

In the previous pages, I have spoken about how your brain works or does not work, and how eating the wrong food can interfere with your mind and then your selling power. All the areas discussed so far, have led to this point.

There are three main areas that either make a person, organisation, or small business rich or keep it poor:

1. Mindset
2. Action and in-action and
3. Flexibility or lack of flexibility in mindset, action, and in-action

The power of the human mind is dynamic and it's a natural, human process for this dynamism to want to grow; it's your inability to see the growth potential that will keep you, your business or your organisation poor.

Life does not often offer easy routes; life is about the journey of discovery and its voyage into the unknown. Your 'Mindset' is the guide on your journey, your rudder if you like.

Mindset is a combination of:

- Your attitude
- Your understanding (or perception) of life's situations
- Your acceptance that things happen and that your journey is to work through difficult situations to find solutions

Mindset

This has forgiveness built into it so that you can move on from past hurts or wounds and heal yourself, making you ready for the next part of your journey. Mindset works constantly so that you can make the most out of every experience and gain the knowledge needed to keep you going and to keep you strong, regardless of the toughness of the journey.

Staying flexible in your thinking allows you to look at every experience (good or bad) as a new chapter in your selling life.

Your Mindset needs to see the positives in every situation: (good or otherwise) and work to make the situation benefit you. Your Mindset can provide you with new horizons and 'breathes fresh air' into your being on-a-daily-basis.

Within your Mindset, you have no room for 'in-action' only 'Action' and Flexibility and Moving Forward.

Your Mindset is the very essence of you, who you are and where you want to go in life from this day forwards. If you feel your Mindset has been holding you back, you can make the changes you want by working with this book.

A negative Mindset will prevent you finding your 'Nuggets of Gold' – this is not only detrimental to how you live and work currently, but it will interfere with every aspect of your future.

Getting your Mindset sorted out will allow you to have unlimited access to every *Mental Nugget of Gold* you possess. The process will allow you to:

- Grow
- Challenge
- Stimulate your thinking and give yourself new and fresh ideas
- See the opportunities where other people do not stay with your challenge
- Ask for help and guidance from your good mind
- Gain the answers you are looking for
- Work with those solutions and
- Have the strength to see even the toughest times through to start at a new beginning

Nugget of Gold Number One – keep your mind flexible and open to new and fresh information

If your mind is steadfast, and inflexible in selling then you diminish your selling power; by keeping you mind open, alert and ever ready for the next strategy that comes you way, you are putting yourself in a powerful position.

(When you are looking at a goal or future target or time, you will need to use a strategy. A strategy is planned action. There is a vast difference between the *opportunistic approach* and taking a planned *strategy in selling.)*

The Difference Between being opportunistic and being a Planned Operator

The opportunistic person is always out there, looking for the easy ride or hoping to get rich quickly without much effort or input on their part. These people buy lottery tickets, play poker machines at the club night after night and week after week and hope '...this week I win something!' They do win from time to time and everyone around seems happy for them, but the money quickly goes and then they start all over again; every time, looking for the next opportunity.

These people are not in control of their own destiny and leaving their life to 'chance' and 'chance' alone. Wouldn't it be wiser for them to put some strategic thinking and planning into their lives so they could at least stay in control, at least some of the time?

To have a 'flutter' and a gamble at times gets the 'juices going' but handing over your destiny to a 'chance happening' doesn't seem very logical when all you have to do is think differently and put some action into your thinking. To think differently does not take much effort and can be done in less than a second!

Case Study 8 – two women's approaches to life

Background

This is a sad case study that shows how two women of the same age work through forty years of their lives.

The Study

Sue met Sarah about forty years ago, just before they both married. Sue went on to have a family: two children, one cat and eventually a dog, and when the kids were old enough, she decided to go to university and gain some awards for the effort she had put into her life. She graduated and then went on to do further research and writing. Sue, says, 'it wasn't easy when the kids were little, we had so little money and we wanted to do so much! Because money was so tight, I simply made the best use of my time and studied to work later in my life'.

Sarah is a different story. She always seemed to have more money than Sue. Sarah had a new home and bought new furniture to put into it, while Sue had only bare wooden floorboards for the first 15 years of her marriage.

Sarah did not work much, a bit of part-time work here and there in a café and some house cleaning. She used her money as 'Pin Money' down at the local club; she went to the club most evenings and spent nearly every weekend playing the poker machines.

Forty years on, Sue loves life, she travels a lot and has seen many different countries. She writes and explores her world. On the other hand, Sarah is still playing the pokies most days and looks much older than her years. If Sarah had a different mindset, her life would be rich and full of opportunity.

Nugget of Gold Number Two – your story

When you are selling for a living you need to attach a story to your product, produce or service – easier said than done, you think? Not so! Stories are with you every day, day in and day out. Because life is one long, continuous story, you forget that within the story of your life, are thousands of short stories – the stories you are living on-a-daily-basis.

A short story told, leaves an impression in the buyer's mind; many years from telling the story, the buyer will remember the story, when they have forgotten what you look like. The story is the 'hook' that fixes you in the buyer's memory bank. You have the opportunity, to make a good impression – do not waste it. Always remember, it's the 'Who' in the image that is important and by connecting your story to your product or service, you are selling, your power is enhanced to dimensions far beyond you and your reach. That is why the story needs to be positive, not negative.

The story needs good content and for the listener to be taken on a journey. The experience of the story is the journey for your customer and is the 'mental hook' and the attraction to your goods, service or produce.

We have only to look to our past, and at mythology and the stories told in ancient times, or at the Aboriginal Elders of Australia, or the North American Indians, to know the power of the story. These knowledgeable people hand-down their history through the stories attached to it – this is the value of the story.

Case Study 9 – If you do not ask, you do not get!

Background

Chris had a dilemma. She wanted to publish a book but needed an image for it and to take it into the marketplace. Because Chris knew a fair bit about marketing, she thought a cuddly possum character would associate or build an iconic image for the new business.

The Study

A year earlier Chris had written a short, children's storybook, which she wanted to publish; she was reluctant to employ an illustrator because of the cost involved. Also, the copyright issue worried her. She searched her mind to find different ways to market the characters and the book. Chris loved to paint, but she had only painted big flowers, flowers full of bright and vibrant colours; they were almost in three dimensions by the time she had put large amounts of acrylic paint onto the canvases.

Being optimistic, she was working on her mind one day and asking herself questions. As she walked up and down pondering her dilemma, an answer came to her: 'paint the illustrations yourself!'

Chris kept quiet about her inner voice. She went home that night, downloaded some animal pictures from the internet and started to draw the outline of a possum. She then went to the garage, found the paint box, and dug around a bit, eventually finding her water colours.
She later looked at the possum's face staring back at her and could not believe what she was looking at.

Chris had discovered a *Nugget of Gold* that could possibly add volumes of interest and revenue to the business of being a writer.

Remember, people buy the stories before they buy the *product* you are selling, it's the image, the impression you give, that makes the difference.

Nugget of Gold Number Three – your 'Compelling Influence'

Compelling Influence is a *Nugget of Gold* that and, as yet, you possibly have not touched. This **Nugget** has been with you for a long time, building and growing from your inception. So now, you are going to discover it.

Ask yourself, *'who are my best friends and why do they stick with me through my life, through thick and thin, good and bad times?'*

If you cannot do that, think of just one person who you admire and with whom you get on very well and then ask 'why, is it, we get along so well?'

Within these questions, are some of the pointers to your third *Nugget of Gold*.

Compelling Influence is part of your uniqueness, it is part of who you are and is one of your skills of survival. *Compelling influence* allows you to live in the community and survive. *Compelling Influence* is not unique to you; everybody has it, but, regrettably, not everybody uses it!

Compelling Influence is the 'glue' that keeps the fabric of our society together. *Compelling influence* includes some of your social bonding within the community. It includes working with the laws of the land so that everybody has a fair chance and lives in a safe environment.

Compelling Influence can be used for both good and bad. However, I am not going to speak about *bad* influence here; I am speaking about your good influence and what you can do with it.

Your *Compelling Influence* carries with it a responsibility on you to use it in a way that is beneficial to you and fits within both ethics and morality. *Compelling Influence* is a gift, and like all gifts it is meant to be beneficial.

So, ask yourself these questions:

- What is it that draws people to me?
- What is it that I do better than anybody else?
- What talents do I have that I can add to, to make me stronger and that I can gain from?

A talent is: your aptitude for doing something different and unique.

A talent is your flair in a medium that feels comfortable to you. Remember, you will naturally go to pick up a paint-brush, or play some tunes on a musical instrument, or write some words on a piece of paper; this flair will naturally 'kick in' and the talent will start working. However, it is your responsibility to find the talent or recognise that you have it; your *Compelling Influence* is connected to one of your talents – you have many talents to be used.

A talent has huge capacity and easily stretches and grows with you as your confidence increases.

A talent is part of the essence and genius of you. A talent is your forte. Whitney Houston has shown how a talent can be larger than our ability to manage it; talents are great gifts, but they need to be *looked after, loved, cherished, nurtured,* and *controlled.*

Now ask:

- What is unique about me?
- What do I have, that I can work with within my Compelling Influence that will make me better at selling, better at life, better at everything I do?

Have you wanted to do something creative or different, but found the doubtful part of your personality condemning these thoughts or ideas before they had time to even surface?

Have you wanted to paint a picture, learn to play the piano, do a course, or learn to ride a bike? Just one thought – 'No, you can't do that,' may be the inner voice that comes back to you. It takes just one negative inner voice to kill your dreams and nobody knows, apart from you, that you are sabotaging your natural gifts and talents and condemning your future.

Your talents are gifts and need to be used, nurtured, and loved.

By denying your talents, you are putting yourself into a *mental black hole* and putting a brick wall up in your thinking; you create a deficit in your mind. So, once again ask:

- What is it that draws people to me?
- What is it that I do better than anybody else?
- What talents do I have that I can add to, to make me stronger and that I can gain from?
- What is unique about me?
- What do I have that I can work with within my Compelling Influence and will make me a better seller, give me the inspiration to keep moving forward and show me the answers that will allow me to work with the situation I am currently in?

I hope you get the message!

Now think, what is my *Compelling Influence?*

How can I use it

- In selling?
- In my life?
- To advance myself in my career
- To get to where I want to go in life
- To enjoy the sun, the rain, the butterflies, and the experiences that makes life rich, purposeful, and fulfilling?

Remember Chris and her painting, she needed desperately to have an image to help in the marketing of her book? Through discovering and working with her *Compelling Influence,* her talent, and the determination to add another dimension and an area of extra possible growth, she developed a bridge which will bring readers to her stories.

Your *Compelling Influence* is yours and yours alone. You can use this Nugget; it's a powerful tool, so please treat it with respect.

Nugget of Gold Number Four – are you working from within a planned thinking process? are you listening to your Messaging Service?

Becoming a *Planned Thinker* is *Nugget of Gold Number Four.* Because you are working in the planning departments of your mind, you become a *Strategic Thinker.*

The *key* to success is in the way you think; everything you do and say comes from a signal from your 'Messaging Service.

So how does your Messaging Service work for you?

In order, to receive complete messages, without interference, you need to think about your brain. Your brain, putting it simply, is the hardware in your computer. Hardware does wear out and does, at times, break down. In order, to build the success strand, you are working on, you need to treat your brain, mind, and body with respect.

When you put plans into place, you are giving your mind directions of where you want to go; you are not allowing the opportunistic part of your personality to take over or be in control. This means you have a strategy to make things happen.

Staying in control of your thinking, taking the actions that are going to give you positive results, all take:

- Planned thinking
- Target setting and
- Staying focused with your eye continuously on the target – you do not have and 'I'll do that later' attitude, or 'I'll start that after the holidays;' a 'Planned Thinker' starts it **'NOW!'**

Make a mental contract with yourself and then write your intentions and targets down as you think of them.

To develop discipline in your life, do the things you do not like doing first and do the pleasurable things last.

So, to make a contract all you need is a piece of paper and a pencil or pen. Now write down your selling goal for one week, then for two weeks, three weeks and a month.

For Example:

Week One: $ or £ 1,000	
Week Two:	1,300
Week Three:	1,500
Week Four:	1,800

Then write down each month for twelve months, slowly increasing the amounts.

Month One:	5,600
Month Two:	7,000
Month Three:	9,000
Month Four:	11,500
Month Five:	14,000

and so on. Continue doing this until you reach the end of year and total up your numbers.

Now work out, how many extra hours, of your own time, you are prepared to put in to develop this new approach. At first, you might put an extra hour a day into the work you are doing; or you might increase this by adding an extra hour's 'ideas time' each day.

By doing these activities, you are sending your mind positive commands and putting yourself on notice to 'take action'. You instantly become sharper in your thinking, and in any product or approach you take to selling.

You know what you are selling and have ideas of its market potential. This, however, is not enough; you need to know the ins and outs of your product, the marketplace, and its maximum market potential. If you are selling food, you need to know the ingredients, the type used, the properties of their potentials. If you are selling real estate, you need to do your background research into the area: who lived there before? Was it a country lane, a farm, a bank building or was the building erected for some purpose other than what it is currently used for? This is building the story, your *Nugget of Gold Number Two.* Even the humble packet of biscuits sitting on the supermarket shelf has a story attached to it.

Nugget of Gold Number Five – establish your authority

Ask yourself these questions:

- Can I do this better than anyone else?
- Are the products I'm selling better than those already in the marketplace?
- Do I offer something extra?
- Can I measure my difference?

You are where you are because you have taken steps to put yourself in that place or position. You may love where you are now or want to change your position, and conditions; you can do all of this, but you need to plan it and then Establish Your Authority.

Establishing Your Authority comes about by being the best in the marketplace; when you are the best, let the public know by telling them; *do not hide your excellence.* Having said this, please remember, also to be humble and assertive when it fits the selling position you are in.

If you are selling something that is completely different to anybody else, it can be difficult to penetrate the market and cut yourself a piece of the market pie. However, if your product is so different, say so: do you say:

'could' 'should' or 'would'

The marketplace is always looking for something different, something unique, whether it is reminiscent of past times such as selling antiques or cutting-edge technology. You do not have to go far to see that some people have insatiable appetites for the latest mobile phone or a piece of technology, while others want old furniture.

The marketplace is as fickle as it is ancient. Fashion and fad are Kings in the market place and, if you are selling, you will understand: last year's colours are unacceptable this year; last year's design is unacceptable this year; last year's label is unacceptable this year!

So, when you are selling for a living it's always:

'I will' – 'I can' – 'I am.'

Nugget of Gold Number Six – creating a unique Selling Proposition based on your market positioning

This is a function of Four points

1)   Your Uniqueness—

Your uniqueness is your branding. There are many stores which sell clothes and shoes but only one 'Nike' brand. It's only the *swoosh*   sign that makes it different and the perception of the brand is its image.

Thousands of businesses make T-shirts and designer trainers, but 'Nike' is still unique in its branding. The same can be said of the McDonald's logo and the branding done by McDonald's marketing department.

2) Your Difference—

Both McDonald's' and Nike are manufacturing, selling products and retailing the world over. However, these two companies can stand alone simply because they have a 'perceived difference'. They are not necessarily different they are just perceived to be different – it is their image that is different.

Within the context of their operations, both of the companies, have been clever in using psychology; they use 'classical conditioning' theory to establish *'....an association between the product and a special feeling...'* (Kaye 1975).

The associations' people perceive between their emotions and particular product/s can be long-term or only have a short existence. However, while the association lasts, there is a commitment and loyalty built between the buyer and the brand.

Your goal in creating *Your Difference* is to build the *Association* between your product or service and your brand.

Selling is pure psychology - simply, if there are no psychological associations with the product, the product will not sell.

3) *Your Specialisation—*

When you specialise in anything you do, you are deliberately making yourself different.

Your specialisation is:

- Concentrated
- Focused and
- Dedicated

You want the world to know, *'this is what I do, and I do it very well.'* Great painters of the past and present have specialised in the way they paint a picture.

Chefs' become focused on one way of creating different and delicious meals.

Dress designers become famous by focusing on a particular cut of the fabric, or by using different combinations of materials to make fashionable clothing; they become famous and some become very wealthy because they have developed a specialisation.

So, what is your specialisation? Once you have identified your *specialisation,* you then need to create the image, the brand and the story attached to the brand and your specialisation.

4) *Your Diversity in the marketplace—*

Having Diversity in the marketplace allows you to make changes, to move with the flow of demands, needs, wants, fashion, attitudes, and current economic situations.

Keeping your business or position 'recession proof' allows you to mix and match your talents, skills, and knowledge to the environment around you. Without diversification in your repertoire of skills and knowledge you are left vulnerable, open to abuse and your market value diminishes very quickly.

- Diversification allows you to move quickly to adjust, move tact to meet the new situation.

Diversification is built through experiencing good, difficult, hard or tough times.

Becoming diversified toughens you up, makes you stronger and allows you to see how to make situations work for you. James Caan once wrote: *'....look at what the market is doing and do the opposite.'* The Real Deal, (2008).

When you become diversified you have:

- A variety of ways to move *up, down, left, right* and so on.

- You can 'multi-skill' and make quick changes to meet your needs.

- You have a range of options that are always available to you and you have created this range through:

1. Taking interest.
2. Listening to and watching what is going on around you.
3. Continuously learning new skills
4. Devoting your time to reading and making sure you stay current with world and local news, and
5. Even when you find some things difficult to understand, you go back and back to it until you can understand at least some of the concepts or ideas - you never give up

Your Diversity in the marketplace shows through because you are willing to:

- Listen to others,
- To take note,
- To think things through,

- When you have a mental picture, you can then make an assumption, of what to do next, and weigh up all of the possibilities and then decide
- What actions to put into place.

A thinking stage may last one or two or five minutes, a week if you are confronted with making a large decision, but do not take too long! After thinking things through, you then take-action. Some people 'think on their feet'; they see a situation, take-action and stay responsible for their situation.

They take hold of the rudder in their life and navigate through the turbulence as well as the good times. This type of activity makes you strong; it gives you diversification and makes you different in the marketplace.

Nugget of Gold Number Seven – understanding motivation and the motivation to buy

I have said, 'selling is a science',' and indeed it is.

Selling is about *understanding your environment. 'what turns people on'* and, *'what's the latest'* not only in fashion, but in the way, people are thinking and behaving? The above, are triggered by individual curiosity, not just your curiosity but the curiosity of the people who want to buy from you. Now ask yourself: 'in my selling situation, what would push their emotional button to buy?'

People have to be motivated to buy. People buy because their senses are prompting them to buy. People buy when they have:

- Cravings
- Yearnings for something different in their lives
- To make themselves feel better
- To give a different personal image and/or
- To intrigue and tantalise other people: 'I have something you don't have!' may be their attitude and the non-verbal message conveyed through the image of what they have bought

Remember, people buy what they want, not what they need; they buy the story!

Possibly, the only exception here is that people will always need food and some dairy products, certain medications, sanitary products, cleaning products and possibly forms of transport.

People decide to buy because of:

- Their emotions
- The story attached to the emotion
- The messages you send out – your communication

There are many reasons why people buy, and it's your job as a seller to get to know *'why a person wants to buy from you?'*

When your customer/s wants to buy from you, you already know they are working with their senses, but they are also internalising the information they have gained:

- *About you*
- *About the item/s you are selling*
- *About the price of your item's and*
- *The benefits to them from the item/s you are selling*

People decide to buy after using their Emotional Intelligence.

They have drawn from:

➢ Past buying experiences which they mentally and internally review.
➢ Benefits gained after buying similar items and
➢ They may be asking their Internal Messaging Service: 'is it worth the money you are asking?

- The emotion 'To Want' – 'To Buy' is personal.
- Choice is a judgement owned by the customer.

- Each person will evaluate, make a judgement on whether to buy or not to buy in their own unique way.

Nugget of Gold Number Eight – Impact and presentation are paramount in selling

Good presentation attracts clients.
Poor or bad presentation loses customers and clients.

Presentation can leave a good impression or a poor one. Good Presentation is:

- ✓ **Image**
- ✓ **Impression and**
- ✓ **Impact**

Good and positive presentation takes continuous effort to maintain. Good presentation is sharp, dynamic, it feels and looks like crystal, it has the edge and vast amounts of energy flowing through it. The colours are usually solid and well defined. Even with lighter, softer colours, there is a good design element throughout the presentation.

Good presentation leaves the viewer with lingering, warm, 'I feel good' thoughts. Good presentation is stimulation and makes the customer or client 'want to buy,' they want more of what you sell.

Good presentation is brought about through careful planning and making finite adjustments to what is presented and how. When goods or services are well presented, they stimulate the *'Pleasure Centre'* in the customer's brain. This stimulation is what leaves the good impression.

Briefly, 'when the neurons of the ventral tegmental area (VTA) of the brain are active and release dopamine to other parts of the brain... the experiences as well as the sensory cues and actions that preceded them will be associated with positive feelings. This identifies research in the neuroscience of addiction.' Linden, *'The Compass of Pleasure,* (2011).

A seller (whether owning their own business or working for an employer) wants customers or clients to be committed to buying from them; to be committed to buying the latest thing they have to offer, whether in men's or women's clothing, make-up, hair colour, motor cars, homes products, produce or services.

Any form of buying which is not buying a need comes from a minor form of:

- Infatuation
- Habit
- Dependence
- Compulsion
- Obsession and/or

- Craving

A created craving or any of the above points can stimulate your brain's *pleasure centre* or that of the customer.

The pleasure of the thoughts connected with what you are selling has been triggered through one of the buyer's senses: seeing, hearing, touching, smelling, or tasting; a sensory experience or from a pleasurable recalled experience.

This experience makes a connection to your customer's *pleasure centre* and stimulates the *'aaaah'* response in the customer.

The *pleasure centre* in your brain combines with the hypothalamus but it is now thought that pleasurable experiences, may come from, a number of different regions, within the human brain. These regions work together and, when stimulated, give you or the customer pleasurable experiences.

When the customer or client's pleasure centre is positively stimulated, the customer will not only buy your products, goods, or services, they will take your message far and wide. Once the impression is stimulated, even in years to come, you will be praised for the impression you have made and the image you have built through being connected to one or more of the customer's senses and then to their pleasure centre.

When the item you are selling carries with it a good:

Image, you have made

Impression and your presentation, has had

Impact

You know you are working positively towards your objective: to sell as many items as possible using both integrity and commitment.

Negative Presentation:

1. **Can Damage**
2. **Can Destroy**
3. **Can Decay**

Once a negative presentation has been made, it leaves a deep impression that is almost impossible to remove from the mind of the recipient. No business wants to leave a 'negative impression' at any time during its life span.

A negative impression can render a business worthless or almost worthless; business is built on:

1. **Customer demand and satisfaction**
2. **Sales to date and the**
3. **Impression for the future**

Positive Presentation

Selling is about positive presentation and impression of every aspect of the business: from a person's appearance:

- The clothes they wear
- The way they comb their hair
- The state of their fingernails
  down to the shoes on their feet, to
- The way the venue is presented (cleanliness)
- The colours of the décor
- The business cards and letter headings
- To the service that is offered.

Positive Presentation is about the way you think and how that thinking leads to your actions.
Positive presentation can:

- ✓ Increase your bottom line
- ✓ Increase your clientele
- ✓ Add benefits to you, your business, your organisation, and your wellbeing
- ✓ Create opportunities where none existed previously, and
- ✓ Improve your cash flow

Nugget of Gold Number Nine

Remember:

Establish your reasons for selling the product or service; establish your authority; establish your Unique Selling Proposition based on positioning; establish your targets; establish the benefits you offer; establish your relationships within the marketplace.

Nugget of Gold Number Ten - working with and identifying your ten nuggets of gold

	YOUR NUGGETS OF GOLD	HOW CAN YOU USE THIS IN THE SELLING YOU DO?
Your Nugget of Gold No 1	Keep your mind flexible and open for new and fresh information	

Your Nugget of Gold No 2	Your Story	
Your Nugget of Gold No 3	Your Compelling Influence	
Your Nugget of Gold No 4	Are you working within a planned thinking process? Are you listening to your Messaging Service?	
Your Nugget of Gold No 5	Establish Your Authority	
Your Nugget of Gold No 6	Creating a unique selling proposition based on your market positioning	

Your Nugget of Gold No 7	Understanding Motivation and The Motivation to Buy	
Your Nugget of Gold No 8	Impact and presentation are paramount in selling	
Your Nugget of Gold No 9	**Remember:** *Establish your reasons for selling the product or service *Establish your authority *Establish your Unique Selling Proposition based on positioning *Establish your targets *Establish the benefits you offer *Establish your relationships within the marketplace	

No business will grow or survive without building relationships – it is your responsibility to build and establish relationships and it means working hard to do this. It is within your competence to bring everything you know and have learned to date, and put it all together to create your own:

'Nugget of Gold - The Package'

Nugget of Gold Number 10

Your Nuggets of Gold need to be:

- ✓ *Influential*
- ✓ *Interesting*
- ✓ *Persuasive*
- ✓ *Powerful and*
- ✓ *Commanding, yet subtle*

Once you are alert and can see where you can modify your behaviours to make things happen, rather than 'waiting for them to happen',' you are in control. When times get tough, working with what you already have and acquiring new skills and a change in your *mindset* will make the difference to your wellbeing and financial survival.

If people only realised, to change is easy – it is the reluctance to change that is difficult and wastes human energy.

Stubbornness, denial, and reluctance kill the human spirit, the human soul and eventually, the human being.

Working on your Nuggets of Gold will help you to get ahead.

To begin with:

Spend 10 minutes a day working on your Nuggets of Gold for the first week.

10 minutes…………………………………………………………….

Then

20 minutes…………………………………………………………….

For the second week

Then

30 minutes……………………………………………………………

For the third week

(It takes six weeks for good or bad habits to form. Working positively with your mind means discipline and working with good habits.)

Your Notes – what can you do to improve the above?

…………………………………………………………………………
…………………………………………………………………………
…………………………………………………………………………

Having your Nuggets of Gold working with you and for you 24/7 is a bonus waiting to be used.

Once people are made aware of the power of their Nuggets of Gold, there isn't any reason why they shouldn't be accountable to make their lives work for them – it takes effort, fortitude, grit, planning and mindset, and, we are nearly all capable of that.

Chapter Seven

Getting To Know Your Brain, Mind And Attitude

The power of the human mind is immense, but it needs to be continually stretched, pulled, worked-on, refreshed, stimulated, and kept in place.

The saying: '...an idle mind is a devil's playground...' is as true in the 21st century as it was when it was originally written in Philippians 4:8.

You and nobody else are the controller of your mind and therefore, if you want to sell for a living, there are certain mechanisms you need to put in place to allow your mind to work at its best.

The illustration above of a human brain and outlined mind will help as you go through this chapter. Anybody can learn to work with their brain and thus their mind.

I have already spoken of the food you eat: your intake of food could be compared to putting diesel in a petrol tank. Many people know the problems that can cause an engine to not start!

But if you do not, once the ignition is turned on, the car may blow clouds of white smoke from the exhaust, and eventually stop running. I am not a mechanic, but there are numerous stories on the internet about diesel being put into petrol tanks!

Taking the wrong food, drink, drugs, or different medication into the human body can likewise bring it grinding to a halt; if you would rather be safe, than sorry with your vehicle, why not with your brain?

If you continually abuse your body and brain, like the vehicle, it will eventually let you down and you will be faced with larger repair bills.

Your body and, further-more, your brain are forgiving, and both respond well to positive treatment and respect, so please, if you are serious about your future, take note of the next few pages.

At the chemical level, food is a primary link to the environment in which you live and the evolution that has taken place over millions of years. The food you eat affects your brain's chemicals that influence your behaviour, your capacity to learn and perform, your thought processes and your emotional reactions to situations. Your food intake dictates and becomes the story of your life.

Diagram 3

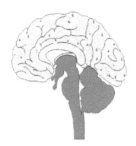

This diagram shows a normally, healthy and functioning human brain.

Each of your customers have a brain, similar to yours - theirs will be working in a similar way but asking different questions.

In order, for the two of you to communicate effectively, there needs to be a 'common ground' a meshing of information. This meshing of information allows you both to feel a degree of satisfaction with the process.

When a customer is buying from you, he or she is not thinking about how their brain is processing the encounter; they are thinking about you and your presentation, and making an evaluation of you, your selling technique and what you are selling. They are asking themselves:

157

- 'Do you appeal to me?' They will continue to analyse you and keep asking the following questions:
- 'Are you also appealing to my emotions?'
- 'Do I need this, or do I want it?' 'Can I buy this another day?' or 'Can I buy this somewhere else?'

The questions running through their mind may even be sub-conscious; they might not even realise the questions they are asking!

When you keep them interested you are continually appealing to their Emotional Intelligence through the information you are sending out and the messages combined with it.

When you are in selling mode, you are communicating to another person and you may even switch you Messaging Service to a higher frequency.

The actual frequency will depend on your sensitivity to the body language and messages you receive back from the buyer. All of this may take place without one word being said. This is why, at all times, you need to maintain your sensitivity to the work of selling.

First, the customer or client needs to connect with you and needs to become familiar with you and your information. Your customer or client will give you their full attention for about three seconds, as previously discussed, and during that window of time, your message needs to be:

- Clear
- Appealing
- Interesting and
- Attention grabbing

For your customer, buying is a sensory experience driven by their emotions. Below is a simple picture of your brain and some of its working areas.

Diagram 4

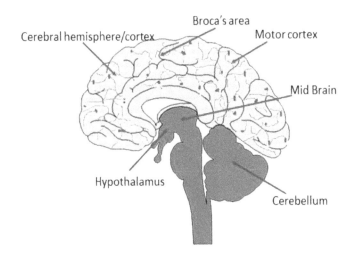

When your brain is stimulated into action, the hypothalamus works in conjunction with other areas of the brain; you are stimulated if you have a prospective customer and the customer is stimulated if you have something to sell that interests them; *therefore,* there is a 'Positive Mental Connection' (PMC) between you.

The brain is a physical structure. It holds millions of *neurons:* a neuron is a nerve cell and is a basic building block both within the brain and throughout the human body.

It is a specialised cell that transmits information within the brain's structure using electrical signals and hormones these make up the chemical messengers. Dendrites are branches connected from the neurons – they carry information to the cell body and away from it towards other neurons, muscles, or gland cells.

When incoming information is received by receptors, (other neurons) with the assistance of hormones, action takes place. This information is then passed down the cell body and on to an axon. The information travels along the axon in the form of an electrical signal known as an 'action potential.'

Once that impulse reaches the end of the axon, the information must be transmitted across the synaptic gap to the dendrites of the adjoining neuron.

Thinking back to the example of the road map and doing a bit of a comparison will give you some idea of the intricate workings of the brain; just a 'blink of your eye' can get your Messaging Service into action.

Going even deeper and taking these ideas further, Eric Berne, the author of *'Games People Play'* and other known books on psychoanalysis, has identified three different roles we all play in every-day life. Berne's ideas are worthy of mention as this will lead me to the mental power you need when selling.

He identified *The Adult, The Parent* and *The Child Ego States* of human personality. Berne's work has been studied in many areas of human behaviour; it has an equally important role in selling.

Without understanding how your own mind is working, how can you even begin to understand how the mind of your customer is working? By taking some time to digest the following information, you are empowering yourself with exclusive mental tools that are continuously at you 'beck and call'. Again, this service, once learnt, costs you nothing but works continuously for you and is available for use twenty-four hours a day, seven days a week.

Because you are now starting to understand how powerful your mind is, you will gain the control you need to make your life completely successful, not just in selling but in every aspect of your life throughout your lifetime.

It has taken me a long time to realise this power, but through continuous research, experience, and writings I now know this is a fact. The power, however, does not come without constant work and vigilance and in some instances, it will cost you something to learn the lessons.

In the diagram below, you can see Berne's three personality types or ego states: *Parent, Adult* and *Child.* Each personality state is a concept that works within the overall paradigm of *Self.*

Diagram 5

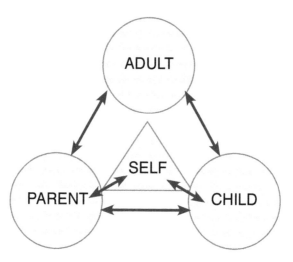

The concept of Self is a fascinating area of psychology - I go deeper into the topic in my book: 'GO' Learn To Drive Your Mind.

Because you are a living, breathing human being, you cannot, at any time during your life escape from *Self*. The 'Self' part of your personality is always with you, night, and day.

Each of us has these interchanging personality ego states working constantly within the brain and interacting in the mind. (Remember, the brain consists of working compartments that form your mind).

The Parent Ego State

Briefly, the Parent Ego State can be loving and caring (LC). This ego state, replays as an adult during parenthood and is shown in caring for your family, your children or your older parents or family members.

PARENT
Ego-Personality
State
Can Become
Dominant &
Dismissive

We own each of these states and we may need to take control, not allowing any one state to become too powerful or too dominant.

When you are selling, you need to show that you care about the client or customer. You also need to understand what their needs are with and for the purchase they are making.

If, say, a person is buying a new piece of technology and you need to show them how to work with it, then you will need to take a more dominant role, but don't become too powerful.

A good measure is to always ask yourself '....*where am I working from on a scale where 1 is submissive and 10 is dominant?*

1 2 3 4 5 6 7 8 9 10

The personality ego state you are enacting at any one time will have different requirements, different tolerances and take you on a different journey.

Case Study 10: Home Should Be Left At Home – while at work - it's time to work

Background

Tanya suddenly found she had more power in a new small business after learning to control her personality states.

The Story

Early one morning, Tanya arrived to do her shift at a recently opened delicatessen. A new colleague, on the earlier shift had arranged the counters and display cabinets differently to how Tanya had left them the day before. Tanya was irritable and started to be rude to the other employees: giving them commands in a gruff tone of voice, not saying please or thank you when they completed a job. She was in a foul mood and everybody knew about it!

The owner of the business was a pleasant man. Not wanting to 'ruffle feathers' or make any of his new employees' feel uncomfortable, he wondered how to cope with Tanya and her mood swings.

He knew Tanya was a good worker and dedicated to his new venture and he wanted to keep her. Her moods and mood swings, however, were extremely difficult to work with, not just for him but also for the other workers in the delicatessen – what a dilemma!

He had an idea and thought about his next move; he wrote the following message on the white board at the back of the delicatessen:

'Dear Ladies

Today is a lovely day and I want you to enjoy your day at work. Please smile and enjoy everything you do, because this one day quickly passes and I want to enjoy working with you all.'

Each woman understood the message. Tanya was letting another side of her personality show and making the workplace a difficult space to work in for everybody else, including the owner of the business.

After a while, it was clear that the message had worked. Tanya and the delicatessen owner had a brief chat about working in a positive environment where everybody is treated with respect and as part of the team.

Later, Tanya was formally made the business manager.

The Adult Ego State

The Adult Ego State is connected to the here-and-now.

When you are working in this personality state you use your past experience and gained knowledge, you own tried, reliable strategies you can put into place when needed and you are constantly testing the reality of your environment. You know what you are doing and will frequently evaluate all the conditions you are working with.

When you work in this personality state, both the Child and Parent demands are integrated and controlled which keeps you thinking logically and in good mental balance. In the workplace, your selling power is increased, and you understand the roles you play, so manage and control them.

People are often described as being mature when they continually work from this state. Maturity is a great gift and allows you to be accountable and responsible for your decisions and actions; to stand up and be counted; to see the 'global picture' of your environment; to experience your grief and hard times; and when you fall, it allows you to rise up and start again.

The Child Ego State

The Child Ego State can become mischievous and uncontrolled when guidelines are not put into place.

CHILD
Ego-Personality
State
can become
mischievous and
dominant

This state may become dominant when you feel your personal power has been taken from you or your true potential is not being recognised. Under the latter conditions, the Adult step to take is to take some positive action to re-create your personal balance and work back into the Adult Ego State.

Finding yourself in a job that is giving little or no satisfaction may allow you to slip into the Child Ego State.

If you are not aware of your personality states, you might find, being in a relationship that takes from you your unique and personal identity, you may slip into and work from the Child Ego State; this can be a very destructive place to be when out of control.

If you can identify with the above, seek some counselling or quietly make some positive changes that are likely to enhance your life, add wellbeing to which, in turn, will allow you to reach your true potential.

Because you are an emotional being, you need to understand your emotional states and how you operate under different circumstances, different life experiences and through different life choices.

At times, you need to work with and connect to the 'Free Child' within the Child Ego State.

The Free Child part of your personality is required when you need to become creative and inventive as in many roles in marketing, graphic design, fashion, hair and design, media, architecture among other careers.

Your Free Child is part of your Child's personality ego state that can become naughty.

Being naughty may take the form of committing crimes, becoming unreasonable and putting extra unachievable demands on other people, including partners in marriage, in love or colleagues in business.

The uncontrolled Free Child is the part of the personality that is always looking for a way out of reality; a person can start abusing drugs or other mind-altering substances when this state is in charge. The Free Child, as an adult, may become angry and feel he or she has been wronged when a child.

The Free Child within the adult may exhibit behaviour which is no longer appropriate in many adult situations; have little or no control, when certain markers or situations present themselves.

I outline two case studies below, one of which (Case Study 11) show the Free Child out of control and the Child Ego State creating almost irreparable damage to a mother – child relationship, and (Case Study 12) identifying how the Child Ego State can 'run amok' when left to run a business.

Case Study 11 – Changes in family Dynamics

Background

Faye had grown up in a stable home environment, but her parents separated when she was in her early teens and now were divorced. Faye could not understand why this should have happened, but she was stuck with both parents living separate lives and living in different towns.

The Story

Faye found the whole situation difficult; her brother and sister seemed to accept it, but she was the youngest sibling and continued to struggle and have difficulty accepting her parents were now divorced.

She could not help but blame her mother for the family breakdown, though Faye had known the marriage had been a difficult one.

Her father had his problems and would drink his way through many situations. Her mother wanted to grow and make changes in her life. She went to college to learn new skills and then on to university.

Faye's parents grew apart and both eventually went in different directions.

Faye was just starting a relationship of her own but there were problems with the new man in her life; he had been married and was separated; he also had two little girls from the marriage.

The girls lived with their mother during the week but spent some weekends with their father. He was a good father and wanted to see as much of his children as he could, so he lived close to them. This relationship too, had problems!

Faye was thinking of going overseas to 'sort her head out' and to see whether the new man was really for her.

After talking to her daughter, Faye's mother, Alice, decided to go to see her one weekend. Alice was worried about her daughter and had found out that Faye, had a few medical problems and did not know whether she might need future surgery; she also had problems with working with her work supervisor. *'These areas: her health, love life and work, seemed to be in turmoil and yet in limbo,'* thought Alice.

Broken marriages, relationship problems, money problems and work problems.

When a person experiences a life crisis, a person who once sold for a living, may find they are unable to sell as they once did.

In different areas of our lives, we experience different areas of stress.

Knowing how your mind works during these times of heavy stress can help you to manage many different areas of your life.

To sell for a living takes a lot of positive, mental, and physical energy. During times of high stress, your body is under attack by the stressful situations you are experiencing, also stress hormones are released. By working with an understanding of how you mentally work, you can learn to put each stressful situation into a compartment in your mind. By isolating each stressful situation or experience, and compartmentalising the situation, you can restore your ability to sell as you once did. Having said this, daily, you will need to do continuous and positive mind work. Saying mantras, such as prayers, songs or poems can help. Like so many people, I have experienced many stressful times in my life and use prayers, I find that saying a prayer gives me positive strength to do the job I need to do. Once I am through the job, I say a prayer of thanks for the guidance I have received.

Faye is learning about how she mentally works, but to mentally grow through her emotional situations will take time, pain, adjustment and restoration.

*****

When there is unresolved anger within an adult, and they revert continuously to memories of their childhood – such a condition creates negative and destructive thoughts which become cruel and destructive actions by the person. This reaction can seriously damage a career path in sales or any work environment.

*****

Negative memories can be managed with maturity and by going to the Adult Ego State. By understanding how the human mind works and taking control of the emotions, most situations can be managed. The pain within Faye is caused by *'the emotion being closely attached to the memory'*. There are techniques that can help with the management of these conditions.

In A Selling Situation

The Free child

The Free Child is a mental state where the person exhibits in-appropriate behaviour in the work environment. The behaviour of the *free child* is paramount to a two-year old tantrum that is exhibited by the adult. This type of behaviour is not acceptable in any form of business or employment. If a person exhibits this type of behaviour, it is advisable for the person to seek professional support.

Case Study 12 – The Free Child

Background

Vera was going to be away for about two weeks.

Christmas was over and it was time to see the family in Victoria, Australia. Her mother was very sick and Vera thought *'…..Mum and I can spend some quality time together'*. The shop had been busy and there was plenty of work for January, so she felt confident that the staff would be kept busy and that cash flow would be maintained.

The Study

Vera left Amy in charge. *'She always seems to do the right thing and gets on well with the customers,'* thought Vera, the business owner.

Arriving back at the shop, she had two shocks waiting for her.

First, the shop interior had been totally re-modelled and not for the better functioning of the shop!

A counter fixed to the wall had been dislodged and moved. The counter had been fixed to allow staff to see the customers as they entered the shop. In its new position, the counter was hidden behind a separation wall - neither the cash register, or counter could be seen while employees were in the workroom prepping flowers or fulfilling orders.

The relocation added to each employee's workload: they would continually be running backwards and forwards to make sure that no customers were left waiting and that the cash register still had money in it!

It was a totally illogical and destructive move by Amy. The counter, now broken and battered, was back in its original place later that day, but the damage to the carpet and wall were not so easily repaired!

The second shock was when Vera discovered that Amy had refunded money for an item already made and approved by a customer. An expensive headdress for a wedding had been created; the item was being kept safe until the bride could pick it up.

Amy had taken it upon herself to talk the bride out of wearing the headdress and then refunded the money for the item.

Designing the headdress, over many months, had required several sittings by the bride. Vera knew the bride well and was working on other areas of the wedding as well as the headdress.

The process of keeping the wedding plans on track had been a slow and carefully thought-out strategy.

In an effort to stamp her own identity on a business owned by another person, Amy had been working from two Ego States: both Parent (showing how she thought Vera should run a business that had been successful for many years) and the Child (moving interior fixtures from a workable position to an illogical and unworkable one, and refunding money the customer the money she had been willing to spend on a purchase she was very happy with.

That afternoon, Amy was encouraged to find another job.

The *Child Personality Ego State* was dominant through the process of refunding the money. It is the Child part of the personality 'getting even' that releases covert destruction in a business, company, or corporation and, in turn, becomes business, company or corporate sabotage.

This type of sabotage happens time and time again in businesses and companies worldwide.

There may be no reason to get even, but because the Child Personality is not at all managed or kept in check by the person or owner of the action, it wants revenge and is possibly seeking 'identity'. Actions of this nature become destructive in any business.

Each, and every day, each one of us uses the Ego States: (Parent, Adult and Child) continuously. It's knowing about and understanding how to manage these Ego States and how they can interact with different foods, drinks, drugs and emotions that is important.

Using the personality states appropriately makes you a winning seller, or indeed, a winner in anything you do. Working with and understanding the power of the personality states is an empowerment process you hold within your mind. Beware: this power can work as easily for your destruction as for great accomplishments, so it needs to be respected and managed with caution and love.

Again, and I repeat, 'it's your management of the Ego States that determines your success. With carefully managed personality states, you can become a powerful player in the marketplace.

The following diagram will help show you how complex your mind can become when you are unaware of how it is working.

Because you can move within your Ego States at great speed, and because different emotions can trigger different emotional states, you will need time to work with the diagram.

In different situations, you might go from Parent to Child back to Adult or from the Child to Adult, Adult to Child - different states will give you different outcomes.

As an adult, the most constructive way of behaving, is within the Adult Ego State and, by continually using this state, you will continue to maintain and create harmony and balance in your life.

It is all very well to see these words on paper, but in order for you to get used to working with your Ego States, you need to test them out.

Testing under controlled conditions can become a lot of fun; you can test yourself:

- While waiting for a bus: start talking to the person standing next to you or
- While you are waiting at the supermarket checkout

Be cautious, however, as you may give unfortunate impressions.

As a rehearsal, you need to continually test, see the outcome, test again, and see the outcome. Testing needs to be done under different conditions and with different people – so play it safe: try a sibling or a good friend.

Diagram 6

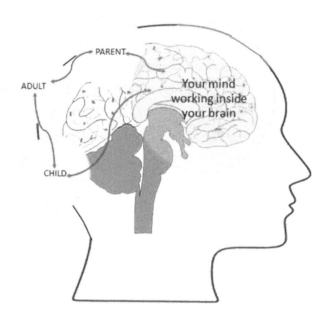

In diagram 6, you can see the internal 'Powerhouse' and how it will enhance your capacity in selling and make your strengths ever stronger. Once you are alert to the differences within your 'Mind Power,' you will continue to hone and refine your skills and to grow mentally stronger; the only person who may possibly stand in your way is you!

As a seller, your responsibility, is to meet the 'wants' and 'needs' of your clients.

From selling a packet of bacon at the delicatessen to selling a Ferrari sports car or a multi-million dollar hotel, when taking on the task of selling, you are working with a mental contract to do your absolute best to conclude the sale.

The more complex the sale, the greater degree of skill you need. You might feel total frustration part-way through a large and complicated sale. The frustration might be the Child Ego State wanting to throw a tantrum but, with the knowledge you now have, you can put that Child back in its place.

You might recall a sale you lost because you or somebody close to you exhibited the Child part of their personality.

Diagram 7

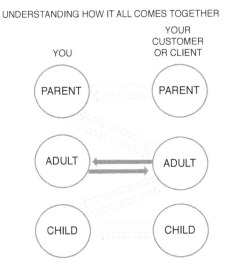

UNDERSTANDING HOW IT ALL COMES TOGETHER

As with diagram 6, both you and the customer or the client go through similar mental movements. However, the difference is the past experiences of both of you and the background knowledge you both have.

Diagram 8

Both people have different life experiences, life expectations, spending capacity, value systems, needs and wants.

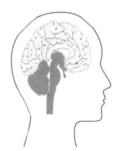

It is when the seller can crossover, find the 'common ground' and work comfortably with the buyer that the transaction takes place.

Emotions combine with your attitude

Attitudes and emotions are vast areas of study and research within psychology; I will only speak of the importance of two areas working in unison to allow you to become effective at your job of selling.

'....attitude is a *"readiness of the psyche to act or react in a certain way"*.' (Jung, 1921). Attitudes very often come in pairs, one conscious and the other subconscious.

The attitude you adopt is initially a thought, on which other thoughts build up as you work through your life. A negative attitude is also a thought, and other incoming and negative thoughts build on it over time. A thought may be conscious or subconscious: however, it is still a thought.

If a person's mindset is negative, a positive environment can be interpreted as a negative one because that person will be looking for the negative aspects within the environment. Their mindset will not necessarily see the good, only the bad or negative within their overall environment at that time.

Each person's personal attitude is elusive; it is important and has a significant bearing on the level of success or failure in life. Each attitude will undergo a degree of change from situation to situation.

Your attitude is connected to your emotions; your attitude is a filter and governs how you see the world, world events and your future. Your attitude shows in the actions you take, in your behaviours and in how you respond to the way you see your experiences and the world events around you.

An Optimistic, positive attitude

It is always your decision: *you have the ability, to choose your attitude.* If your decision is to have an optimistic and positive attitude in life, you will practise positive self-talk daily. Your optimistic and positive attitude is dominant and creates positive mental habits, which include always seeing the glass 'half-full,' not 'half-empty.'

You will always give people the benefit of the doubt, and always have a sense of hope and trust that things will turn out okay and for the better as time passes.

With an optimistic attitude and a mindset that likewise is positive and compassionate, you have hope and trust built in. You will be driven to take certain beneficial actions – actions that are not only beneficial to you but to the world around you.

Through such an attitude and mindset, you become more relaxed, carry less stress in your body and on your mind, you are giving and sharing and are competent in the things you do.

You become healthier and have a healthy level of confidence. You might try something new and know, '...that even if it doesn't work as you anticipated there is always something new to be gained through your endeavour and experience.'

Your confidence tells you that everything will work out for the best because you know there is always a window opening or a new insight within the endeavours you have undertaken.

If selling has been difficult for you, take some time out and think about an area in which you have experienced success. Your success would have required you to decide how you were going to act and behave when in that situation.

Back-track and try to recall your emotions at that time and the attitude you had, then do some emotional recall; write it down and reflect on how you felt.

Within a positive attitude control is centred within you, not outside in your environment. If you have determined a positive outcome for your work and selling, you have determined the outcome before the circumstances or events even started – you are *forewarned and forearmed.*

To know how you are going to respond in your environment is extremely powerful and a positive attitude is fundamental to your success.

Positive attitude includes positive thinking and action

Diagram 9

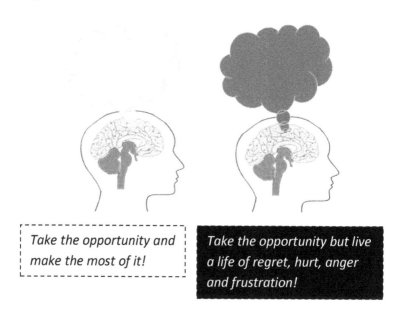

Take the opportunity and make the most of it!

Take the opportunity but live a life of regret, hurt, anger and frustration!

You have the choice: even in dire circumstances, you can make something work and start again! Or you can choose to live a life of unfulfilled anger and frustration.

Your attitude is attached to your emotion and emotion has a feeling attached to it. When you feel frustrated, anxious, sad or angry, you feel uncomfortable and you want the feeling to quickly go away.

Case Study 13 – Failure to learn from the past

Background

Liz was twenty years old and had been looking for work for a long time. She had moved from the country and had previously had a drug problem. After going to rehabilitation, she thought she was managing her condition well. Then she found a job working in a pub – the first job in about a year.

The Story

She was aware she could 'go off the handle' quickly but she was enjoying the work and liked the women she was working with. Liz liked Paul and Etty, the husband and wife team that owned the pub and thought she would be there for a long time. She knew she needed other things in her life and had been thinking about going to college. She 'could think about these things now she was working!' she thought.

One night she and her boyfriend decided to go their own ways. She felt bad about this.

The next morning when she arrived at work, she felt irritable and frustrated at the boyfriend situation and she brought her feelings with her.

Etty, was at the bar talking to another staff member about moving the business forward with some new stock and new ideas.

There were just the three of them. Liz felt her mind going in different directions; she was not coping with the conversation and started to get irritable.

Before she knew it, she was out of control and giving the boss a 'right mouthful'. When she had finished her abuse, she picked up her bag and headed out of the pub doorway, never to be seen by Paul or Etty again. And Liz did it all to herself.

She was now out of work, her relationship with her boyfriend had broken down and her dreams of going to college were left in shreds. A difficult situation when drugs have interfered with the workings of the brain which in turn damage the brain's Messaging Service and the Child Ego Personality State takes over.

Liz could have managed her situation. She needed to prepare herself for work that day; she could have gone for a walk, done some exercises, had a cry or pounded the pillow; but it is not wise to 'verbally be rude to the boss, who's paying your wages.

In this case study, we can see how drugs have worked with Liz's personality states.

When such negative interference destroys the good prospects of your life, you are reduced to 'Zero' and the only option you have is to start again. Rebuild, refocus, and learn from the last lesson or mistake.

People who become out of control and who do not understand what is going on inside their heads will and do revert to mind-altering substances, after all, it is an easy way out of reality. Other areas used to ease the pain are excessive spending or shopping.

Although, strength can be gained through the experience, if the lesson is not learned, the journey becomes more difficult each time. It is far easier, to work with your brain, understand your mind and take control of your ego states and tell them what you want to do and the actions you want to take. After all, your future depends on you.

The only way to heal emotional distress is to work with the situation and feel the pain.

With her negative attitude at the time, Liz walked out of her job, she would have felt:

- Powerful
- Vague
- Formless
- Indistinct
- Unclear

- Fuzzy
- Blurred
- Indistinguishable
- Indefinite and possibly
- Ambiguous

Feelings can hurt you deeply. The magic that you now know is that feelings, thoughts, and behaviours are all related to each other – change one, and the others will follow.

Thoughts are easier to change than feelings and behaviours.

If you feel your attitude is holding you back, you have the power to change your thinking.

By changing what you *think,* you will change what you *do,* this will change the emotion attached to what you *feel* and you will create a resiliency and strength in your life.

You have worked with your attitude to get it to where it is today. If you are unhappy with your selling power, examine and measure your attitude; use your attitude for the greater good, treat it with respect and use it wisely.

Hippocrates once said:

'men ought to know that from nothing else, but the brain comes joys, delights, laughter and sports, and sorrows, grief, despondency, and lamentations...'

Getting to know and accept you have a good brain and mind can sometimes be difficult to do. Many students find, once they acknowledge they have a brain and mind and they start to consciously work with them, a whole new and exciting world opens-up before their very eyes.

With the information you have read so far, make some positive notes about the points you've discovered and the benefits you are starting to experience in your life.

Your Notes

....

....

....

....

....

....

....

....

Getting to know your brain, mind and attitude is a long journey that gives you powerful learning and ensures your future.

There are no shortcuts – the journey is the journey and if you want to be the best in your field, it's up to you to take on the challenge and learn all you can to gain the advantages.

Chapter Eight

Discovering Your Unique Selling Power – Your Centre of Intelligence Discovered

You have only uncovered a minuscule amount of knowledge to date. However, your mental tools are in place and it is time to start building from the foundations of your knowledge.

Going a little deeper and adding to the words written so far, you need to bring this whole package together.

There are several reasons why you have read this book and I hope your primary reason is to add depth, satisfaction and fulfilment to your career and to enrich your life with the knowledge you've gained so far. You are still on your pathway of learning, so please do not ever give up:

- You need to know more about selling!
- You want to gain financial independence!
- You want to be the best in your field!
- You know you have more but have been struggling to find out where your full mental capacity can take you!
- You know and want to create more of everything in your life - from:

- ✓ Feeling secure

- ✓ Being able to 'stand on your own two feet.'

- ✓ Having the answers to the questions asked at the right time

- ✓ Being able to accept new challenges without the fear of failure

- ✓ Always being able to turn your hand to the next venture without feeling intimidated

- ✓ Finding solutions to problems when others have not been able to do so.

- ✓ You are now able to define and work with your own destiny
- ✓ You now think clearly and know the success you want
- ✓ You now have the 'mental power' to work with difficult situations, including selling, and achieve the best outcome, which usually includes winning the deal
- ✓ Through the mental hard work you do you are now pre-determined to win because you have flexibility in your thinking and look for the 'Win-Win' situation

- ✓ **If you feel you cannot meet the criteria the first time, you now have the inner strength to work hard, face the situation and come back a second time**
- ✓ **You also want the time to live your life and now know how you want to live it with family, loved ones and friends**
- ✓ **You now want to pursue life-long dreams and the time to enjoy them.**

Your mind has the ability to do all of the above but you need to work with your mind and ask the questions you want answered – 'if you don't ask, you don't get!'

Case Study 14 – Missed opportunities!

Background

Florence had always spoken about writing a book on the settlement of Sydney, Australia. She had lived through two world wars, the construction of the Sydney Harbour Bridge and of other significant Sydney buildings and she knew a lot about her native city.

The Story

Florence was a kind and loving grandmother and had lived in Sydney her entire life. She recalls, '...when I was a girl growing up around here, there were only fields. We lived in the house on the back, over there!' She points to the back fence, only about six metres away. She continues, 'we were so poor! My mum had thirteen children and not much money, but I tell you, were those floors clean? They were only hard mud floors, but they were as clean as clean!' She thinks a little more, recalling her childhood over seventy years before.

In many other conversations, Florence said, 'I should write a book about early Sydney.'

Sadly, she died not long after the last conversation and not one word has been written down until now.

No one person is ever left without experiences in life. How you or anybody else works with life experiences and records those experiences is a matter of personal preference.

Some experiences leave people traumatised and needing help to work through and heal them. Others take a relatively minor trauma and make a 'mountain' out of it. How we each internalise the incoming information and knowledge is all a matter of choice.

I write because I know that through writing, the words can help and support other people. My words are only building blocks to be used by you; you read them now and work on them; you might modify them later and develop ideas from those thoughts and words and possibly into your future. My words, I hope, will give you the mental tools you need to add quality to your life and future.

My work has only come together, because I have also learnt from experiences and then written about the experience. I have also learnt that leaving life 'to chance' is not an option even if I call upon 'Divine Intervention,' I still need to show a lot of initiative and put in the hard work.

As I've written, more and more information and as it is revealed to me – one lot of writing seems to open the door to the next writing to be done.

I learn more techniques and gain extra knowledge through the research I do and then I ask more questions and so the journey continues. I continually ask more questions of my mind and as the questions are answered another question emerges. I then put the information down on paper and it becomes a book.

Education is a fascinating area and I will continue exploring it and using the exploration as a tool or gift to write more books. I am not the only person interested in the human brain and how it works: there are many eminent scientists working on the brain, who are also looking for answers.

Earlier in the book, I have already suggested that the human mind cannot be photographed. To take this idea a bit further: if for instance, you are thinking of painting your house, you might see a nice gleaming picture of your freshly painted house in your mind; to date, there isn't a camera or piece of technology that can extract that picture of your newly painted house from your mind. You are the only one who holds the picture in your head.

With the use of CAT scans, the human brain and its activities can be photographed. The energy transmitted through a person thinking is recorded on a graph and the thought pattern is monitored.

The CAT scanner can take painless pictures of slices of the brain: your brain is releasing a pulse that is monitored and recorded. However, it cannot see the 'mind picture' of your freshly painted house.

You need mind pictures to keep you going. Mind pictures assist you to reach your goal. Your pictures are yours and yours alone and nobody can take them from you.

This book was a 'mind picture' at one time. It was an, *'I need to do that'* on my To Do List!' The words in this book are meant to be used as tools and I am not saying this book 'fixes all,' it does not, but it is at least three-quarters of the way there.

You need strategies and plans in life. You do not need tactics, get-rich-quick internet ideas, or magic, gossip or somebody else's dream. Your mind has enough power to create your own dream, and you have the ability, to bring the dream into reality.

You need to take positive action and put extra energy into your dreams and plans, and you need to keep 'topping up' the energy with positive thoughts, actions, and future-plans. By working with the above information, you will become aware of your 'Centre of Intelligence'. Your 'Centre of Intelligence' is the ultimate 'Powerhouse' of your collected:

- Life experiences
- Life skills
- Life knowledge
- Life emotions and dreams
- Life talents
- Life resources
- Life strengths
- Life training
- Life opportunities and
- Life passion

Discovering Your *Centre of Intelligence*

Your *Centre of Intelligence* is within you. It goes nowhere and does nothing until you work with it. Your 'Centre of Intelligence' is always hungry for knowledge and experience. Your 'Centre of Intelligence' is the pivot of you and your life rotates around it; it is the kernel or seed that wants to be continually nurtured to grow stronger and stronger. Your 'Centre of Intelligence' is your universal gift and, if you deny this gift, you will live a life of unfulfilled frustration and die asking the question *'why was I put on this earth?'*

There is always a reason and purpose for a person's existence – as in the case of the grandmother above, who did not write the book she had always spoken of writing.

Your 'Centre of Intelligence' is the genius in you. The Centre of Intelligence includes your natural and inherited instinct.

Natural-Instinct

This is a direct descendant from your ancestors and lives within the 'old brain' or 'reptilian brain' – your cerebellum. Your cerebellum allows you to walk without falling over. Its system refines your gross motor skill (moving your arms, legs and other heavy joints), it sends you messages through your senses when you are walking into danger; it tells you to run faster, hide, take shelter or gives you the warning: BEWARE all is not well here!'

Messages from your cerebellum will tell you when someone is lying to you. It's messages will come when the 'hairs on the back of your neck stand up,' which results in you taking note of the situation and feeling uncomfortable with how another person is acting or what they are telling you.

The cerebellum carries stored messages from your ancestors within your DNA. It may even carry footprints of information that was learnt thousands of years ago and has now been handed down to you.

The cerebellum is believed to be part of your subconscious mind and is awake 24/7 and works for you and, you, alone. It receives and sends out messages, stores information and discards other information.

The 'old reptilian brain' (your cerebellum) is your best friend, use it; it too, needs exercise and workouts. Keep feeding it with good information and do not stop asking it questions. The cerebellum, I believe, holds the key to many of life's gifts (untapped or otherwise!) and the answers to many of life's crisis.

Your left and right cerebral cortex work with your cerebellum and each interacts and interconnects with the information you receive via your senses; each plays its role in your survival, your wellbeing and the roles you take in life.

In all of the above, you are working with the information which is being transmitted to you through your senses.

Your brain has millions of electrical currents running through it. The circuitry contains neurons and hormones that hold genetic information for other cells. Neurons pass information, from one neuron to the next. The information is transferred through hormones and electrical pulses. I have mentioned this in a previous chapter. Just to reinforce this information, 'the information is passed down the cell body to the axons and is your message to take action', this is your 'action potential'. 'Action potential' is an electronic message to kick a ball, write a letter, make a phone call, attend a course, go on to higher education or sell more!

Do you remember the story of Chris and how she learnt to paint animals' over-night? I believe this was her old reptilian brain working; it could even be part of a latent talent unfolding, or a gift handed down from an ancestor.

Chris was receiving signals sending her information; this information was picked up by her left and right hemispheres and she did what she was told: 'do it yourself!'

Chris was working from her 'Centre of Intelligence' which is the place you should work from. Chris had the information within her brain to paint animal pictures, then her mind was put to work and she had the courage to pick up some latent talent, she put the talents to work and produced two small children's books.

Your Centre of Intelligence has collected and stored information and this is waiting to be used; it is constantly at your disposal. Your Centre of Intelligence is working with the components of your mind, and the electrical circuitry in your brain.

Your Centre of Intelligence holds within it: your past learning and skills, your resources, your strengths, your matured talents and your past-experience, and expertise.

You will add to your Centre of Intelligence re-learned information and skills, new mental tools that you develop and future incoming information that will include: your future growth and your choices.

By taking each part of your Centre of Intelligence separately, you will understand how this framework comes together.

You will only get to know your Centre of Intelligence by identifying the areas of strength you have. Do not waste time on your weaknesses; weak spots become stronger as you become stronger. Spending time trying to develop a weakness into a strength that is not natural to you will delay your progress, cause you frustration and anger you and invariably, you will give up and not come back to what is naturally yours and yours alone.

Diagram 10 Your *Centre of Intelligence*

This consists of four main components:

Your Centre of Intelligence is where your life-long learning and intuition meet and work for you.

Your Centre of Intelligence works 24/7 and never takes a holiday!

Your Centre of Intelligence is the 'locus' of who you are and is your genius and is always waiting for you to switch the switch to **'ON'**. If you do not switch on the light, you will live in your own created darkness.

Your Centre of Intelligence is your cognitive ability and your comprehension of experiences and life situations. Your cognition is the combination of your electrical wiring and your technology and is always under construction, from adding new skills and understanding to past experiences and positively held beliefs.

You advance and become familiar with each new encounter; you take on the challenge and grow with the energy that allows you to start each day as a new beginning.

Because of your alertness to your direction and how your mind is working, your base continually becomes stronger.

Your Centre of Intelligence is always working with you – day and night. It's at this point you start to realise just how powerful your human mind is.

Your Centre of Intelligence is the very 'kernel' or 'essence' of you. It holds within it your:

- Wishes
- Dreams
- Plans
- Desires
- Goals
- Your future in a (selling) career or career and
- Your future and direction in your life

By working with your Centre of Intelligence you can achieve your highest goals or dreams.

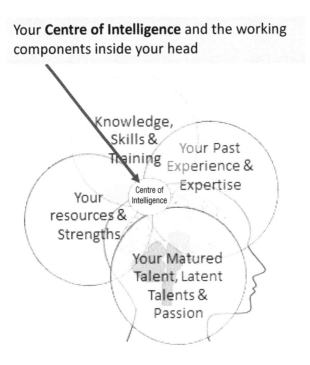

Your **Centre of Intelligence** and the working components inside your head

Knowledge, Skills & Training

Your Past Experience & Expertise

Centre of Intelligence

Your resources & Strengths

Your Matured Talent, Latent Talents & Passion

Signposts

To begin with, you need to develop some support systems; this can be done through identifying the signposts you will need to follow. Each of the following should be scored out of ten. If your score is below five, you need to concentrate on that area to strengthen it; it is not a weakness, it is an area of your life waiting to grow. Follow the simple steps below and do the exercise.

First: Identify your resources and strengths; don't even consider your weaknesses.

Identify your resources and strengths and assess them.

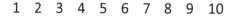

1 2 3 4 5 6 7 8 9 10

Second: Identify your talents and your passion – do not do what everybody else is doing, follow your passion – it's your journey!

Identify your talents and your passion and assess them.

1 2 3 4 5 6 7 8 9 10

Third: List your resources, your skills and training this is the knowledge you have.

List your resources and assess them

1 2 3 4 5 6 7 8 9 10

Fourth: List your experience and your expertise.

List your experience and your expertise in as many areas as you can and assess them.

1 2 3 4 5 6 7 8 9 10

By identifying your strengths, you are on the 'fast track' to a powerful career in selling.

From the previous page above:

- Isolate your strengths.
- Play to win.
- Be completely clear and only work on what is essential in your career and selling.

1. Identify your talents and your passion. Stay focused, do not take your eye off your target or the game.
2. Obstacles are manageable and are only temporary.
3. Identify your experience and expertise.

When you understand how your environment can and does affect your income, lifestyle, future and your potential, doesn't it make sense to look after your brain and mind and to take the time to get to know the power you hold within your head - the Power of your **Centre of Intelligence?'**

The most exciting part of writing this book was coming to this end chapter. To bring together my years of research in identifying the unique and individual 'Centre of Intelligence' has been an exciting breakthrough in human psychology; it makes the sense and the amount of work done to-date so worthwhile.

You have invested time, money, and energy to get to this point, please keep working with your gained knowledge to add richness and fulfilment to your life.

Your Notes

....

....

....

....

....

....

The journey into success is fascinating and becomes even more so as you work with your brain and mind.
The fascination for me: everybody has the capabilities of becoming successful, but few will put in the effort, which is required to make the difference, please do not let it be you.

Your Notes

Your Notes

....

....

....

....

....

....

....

....

....

....

....

....

....

....

....

....

....

From the author

It has taken over forty years to put this book together. No, I haven't written this book over these years, but I have been working with my *'Centre of Intelligence,'* which has allowed me to collect the information to put this book together, now in 2012, 2013 and 2020.

There has been a lot of pain on the way and the journey has been one of sheer hard work, some of which contributes to the combination of the written words.

I hope my journey adds to the quality of your life and your journey. If you are in a *'hard or difficult place'* at the moment, I send you my good thoughts and say to you, *'never, never give up'* – when you work with your brain and mind, it will reveal many answers.

The process, the journey has many benefits to offer, even in hard times. A child's smile and the colours of a butterfly's wings can bring a change into your life.

Your 'Centre of Intelligence' is a gift of un-paralleled proportions and belongs to you.

I have worked with young people who have been on drug rehabilitation programs and seen the pain in their faces because they did not know or understand the gift they have inside their heads. I have also taught in the jail and young offenders' institution gathering research information. Sadly, and without the knowledge you now have, these people had unwittingly abused their inherited gifts.

While the above experiences have given me insight, as I have mentioned at the beginning of the book, I have given my ideas to other people who had invested in a new business for $700,000 and later sold at $3 million. Without the previous work I have done, I could not share this information with you.

My strengths now come in the books I write and, if my writing is supporting you on your journey, I have met some of my goals.

Thank you for buying this book. Ten percent of the net proceeds will be contributed to Diabetes Australia for continued research into Type One, Juvenile Onset Diabetes and Cancer Research.

Christine Thompson-Wells

Bibliography:

Bekerian, D.A. & A.D. Baddeley, (1980) 'Saturation advertising and the repetition effect' *Journal of Verbal Learning and Verbal Behaviour,* Vol 19, pp.17-25.

Berne, E.(1964) *'The Games People Play,'* Grove/Atlantic, Inc., New York.

Brean, H. (1958) 'What hidden sell is all about', *Life*, March 31, pp - 104-114.

Caan, J. (2010) *The Real Deal*, Virgin Books, Random House, London.

Cardwell, M.C., Clark, E. & Meldrum, C (1996) *Psychology For A Level,* Collins Educational, United Kingdom.

Cialdini R. B. (2001). 'The science of persuasion'. *Scientific American.*

Cohen, D. (1979) J.B. Watson: *The Founder of Behaviourism*, Routledge, London

Elliot J. (1984).'How advertising on milk bottles increased consumption of Kellogg's Corn Flakes', in Broadbent, S (1984) Twenty Case Histories, Holt, Rinehart, Winston, Boston.

Ehrlich, D et al (1957) Post decision exposure to relevant information', Journal of Abnormal and Social Psychology, Vol.54, pp 98-102.

Festinger, L. (1957) *A Theory of Cognitive Dissonance*, Harper & Row, <u>New York.</u>

Gardner, H. (1983) *Frames of Mind*: The Theory of Multiple Intelligences, Basic Books, New York.

Goleman, D. (1996) *Working With Emotional Intelligence Bloomsbury,* London.

Horowitz, I.A. & Kaye, R.S. (1975) 'Perception and advertising', *Journal of Advertising Research,* Vol. 15, pp.15-21.
Jung, C. (1964 edn) *Man and his Symbols*, London: Aldus-Jupiter Books, <u>London</u>.

Keller, K.L. (1987) 'Memory factors in advertising: the effect of advertising retrieval cues on brand evaluation*, Journal of Customer Research,* Vol.14, pp 316-333.

Koob, A.(2009) *'The Root of Thought.'* FT Press, Pearson Education, Upper Saddle River, New Jersey.

Linden, D. (2011) *'The Compass of Pleasure,'* Penguin USA New York.

MacLean P.D. (1973) *'A Triune Concept of Brain And Behaviour'* University Press of Toronto, Canada.

MacLean P.D. (1982) *'On the progression evolution of the triune Brain,* In E. Armstrong & D. Falk (eds). *'Primate Brain Evolution',* Plenum Press, New York.

Mullen, B. & Johnson, C. (1990) *'The Psychology of Customer Behaviour,* Erlbaum, Hillsdale, New Jersey.

Payne, W. (1985) *'A Study of Emotion – Developing 'Emotional Intelligence''* Doctorial Thesis.
Philippians 4:8 'An Idle Mind Is the Devil's plaything.'

Salovey, P. & Mayer J.D. (1990). *'Emotional Intelligence'. Imagination, Cognition, and Personality*, 9, 185-211.

Stayman, D.R. & Batra, R. (1991) 'Encoding and retrieval of ad affect in memory', *Journal of Marketing Research,* Vol. 28, pp232-239.

Thompson, G.E. (1984) 'Post-it notes click thanks to entrepreneurial spirit', *Marketing News*, Vol. 18, pp. 21-23.
Thorndike R.K. (1920) Charles Darwin. 'Intelligence and Its Uses', *Harper's Magazine* 140, 227-335.

Thorndike E.L. (1898) 'Animal Intelligence: An experimental study of the associative processes in animals'. *Psychological Review* Monograph Supplement 2 (Whole No 8).

Wechsler, D.(1940). 'Non-intellective factors in general intelligence'. *Psychological Bulletin, 37,* 444-445. USA.

Watson, J.B. & Rayner R. (1920) 'Conditional Emotional Reactions.' *Journal of Experimental Psychology,* Vol 3, pp 1-14.
Other Research
http://www.fi.edu/learn/brain/fats.html

Printed and produced by Books For Reading On Line.Com, Australia for www.booksforreadingonline.com under license from MSI Australia

Lightning Source UK Ltd.
Milton Keynes UK
UKHW021308050321
379827UK00007B/227